BTEC Tech Award
Sport

Student Book

The publisher gratefully acknowledges the permission of copyright holders to reproduce copyright material.

Cover image: (c) Lukasz Libuszewski/Shutterstock.com

All other image credits are listed at the end of the book.

Every effort has been made to trace copyright holders and to obtain their permission for the use of copyright material. The publisher will be glad to make arrangements with any copyright holder it has not been possible to contact.

Copyright © 2023 Eboru Publishing

All rights reserved. No part of this publication may be reproduced, distributed, or transmitted in any form or by any means, including photocopying, recording, or other electronic or mechanical methods, without the prior written permission of the publisher, or under licence from the Copyright Licensing Agency. See www.cla.co.uk for more details.

First edition 2023. Impression 10 9 8 7 6 5 4 3 2 1

ISBN 978-0-9929002-7-4

Whilst every effort has been made to ensure all information in this book is correct, the publisher shall not be liable for any loss of profit or any other commercial damages, including but not limited to special, incidental, consequential, personal, or other damages, due to any information or advice contained in this book.

If you do spot any errors in this book you can alert the publisher at: enquiries@eboru.com

Ordering Information

Special discounts are available for class set purchases by schools, colleges and others. For details, contact the publisher at: orders@eboru.com

Trade orders: copies of this book are available through the normal wholesalers. For any queries please contact: orders@eboru.com

www.eboru.com

Features in this book

Intro
A very short ice-breaker activity, to start the lesson or topic

Vocab
Difficult or unusual words are defined

A1 Components of physical fitness

Aerobic endurance

The human body needs energy to move. One way we get energy is by using oxygen to break down food.

Our bodies use the **cardiorespiratory** system to transfer oxygen from the air to our cells.

The cardiorespiratory system is made up of the heart and lungs, blood and blood vessels.

When we breathe in, we send oxygen to all the cells in our body

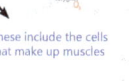

These include the cells that make up muscles

Intro
With a partner, take it in turns for one person to jog gently on the spot whilst the other person times them for 1 minute. How long does it take for your breathing to get quicker?

cardio relating to the heart
respiratory relating to breathing
aerobic using oxygen

The cardiorespiratory system also removes waste products from our cells

The cells use this oxygen to release energy, which can move our muscles

Cardio relates to the 'heart' and respiratory relates to 'breathing'.

When our bodies get energy using oxygen we call it aerobic. Aerobic means 'using oxygen'.

The cardiorespiratory system provides enough oxygen so that:
- muscles can move at a low or medium level of intensity
- muscles can keep working at this intensity for quite a long time.

Aerobic endurance is how long we can keep performing at a low or medium level of intensity. Aerobic endurance is important for any activity that takes place for more than around 30–90 seconds.

You can tell when an activity is testing your aerobic endurance, because you will begin to feel out of breath.

Aerobic endurance depends on how good the cardiorespiratory system is at getting oxygen to the muscles.

Professional athletes have an excellent cardiorespiratory system. They can perform at a higher intensity, for longer.

This professional marathon runner has a very high aerobic endurance. He can run very fast for more than two hours without stopping.

Muscular endurance

Muscular endurance means how long your muscles can keep working for at low or medium intensity. Muscular endurance is not the same as muscular strength – for that see the next page.

To understand muscular endurance, consider an activity such as a plank. Many people find it hard to do a plank for long. At a certain point the stomach and arm muscles can no longer hold the body's weight.

Notice that you don't stop a plank because of aerobic endurance – you are not out of breath. It is because the muscle cannot physically take it any more.

A plank requires good muscular endurance rather than aerobic endurance

Muscular endurance allows you to use a muscle at low or medium intensity for quite a long period of time. It is important in many sports and physical activities. For instance, muscular endurance is important for:
- kicking a ball in a football or rugby match
- serving throughout a long tennis match
- supporting the body's weight when rock climbing.

There are many different muscles in the human body. Muscular endurance is different for different groups of muscles. For instance:
- a professional rower has excellent muscular endurance in their arms, shoulders and back
- a professional cyclist has excellent muscular endurance in their legs and buttocks.

Muscular endurance can be measured by how many exercise repetitions someone can do, rather than the heaviest weight they can lift or move.

Activity
1. List i) one team sport, ii) one individual sport, and iii) one activity, where aerobic endurance is important.
2. List i) one team sport, ii) one individual sport, and iii) one activity, where muscular endurance is important.
3. a) Explain why aerobic endurance is important for a football player.
   b) Explain the impact of aerobic endurance on the performance of a football player.
4. a) Explain why a tennis player needs to have muscular endurance.
   b) Explain the impact of muscular endurance on a tennis player's performance.

Key terms
Important terms are highlighted in **bold**

Activity
Questions at the end of each spread or topic test your knowledge and understanding

Link
Highlights connections between different topics or components.

See Component 2 LOA for more on aerobic endurance

Contents

Features in this book   3

Component 1 Preparing participants to take part in sport and physical activity   7

A1 Types of providers of sport and physical exercise   8

A2 Types and needs of sport and physical activity participants   20

A3 & A4 Barriers to participation and ways to remove barriers for different participants   24

B1 Different types of sports clothing and equipment for participation   28

B2 Technology benefits to improve participation and performance   37

B3 The limitations of using technology in sport and physical activity   45

C1 Planning a warm-up   48

C2 Adapting a warm-up for different types of participants and physical activities   58

C3 Delivering a warm-up to prepare participants for physical activities   62

Component 2 Taking part and improving other participants' sporting performance   67

A1 Components of physical fitness   68

A2 Components of skill-related fitness   74

B1 Techniques, strategies and fitness for sports   80

B2 Officials in sport   88

B3 Rules and regulations in sport   94

C1 Planning drills and conditioned practices to develop participants' sporting skills   110

C2 Drills to improve sporting performance   116

Component 3 Developing fitness to improve other participants' performance in sport and physical activity   121

A1 The importance of fitness for successful participation in sport   122

A2 Fitness training principles   126

A3 Exercise intensity   128

B1 Importance of fitness testing   134

B2 Fitness tests – aerobic endurance   140

B2 Fitness tests – muscular endurance   144

B2 Fitness tests – flexibility   147

B2 Fitness tests – speed   150

B2 Fitness tests – muscular strength   152

B2 Fitness tests – body composition   154

B3 Fitness tests – agility   158

B3 Fitness tests – balance   160

B3 Fitness tests – coordination   162

B3 Fitness tests – power   164

B3 Fitness tests – reaction time   167

B4 Interpretation of fitness test results   168

C1 Requirements for fitness training methods   170

C2 Fitness training methods for physical components of fitness   172

C3 Fitness training methods for skill-related components of fitness   178

C4 Advantages and disadvantages of each fitness training method   182

C5 Provision for taking part in fitness training methods   191

C6 The effects of long-term fitness training on the body systems   194

D1 Personal information to aid training fitness programme design   200

D2 Fitness programme design   201

D3 Motivational techniques for fitness programming   204

Normative data   208

Index   213

While this book is designed to help and support teachers and learners throughout the course, the only official source of information about the qualification is the qualification specification, published by the awarding organisation. Teachers delivering this qualification should always refer to the specification for definitive information about all aspects of this qualification.

The questions in this book are designed to help learners develop their knowledge, skills and understanding. They are not assessment questions. Please refer to the awarding organisation's guidance on assessment.

Component 1 Preparing participants to take part in sport and physical activity

In this component you will learn about:
- The difference between sport, physical activity and outdoor activities
- Different types of provision of sport and physical activity
- Barriers to participation for different people and how they can be overcome
- Sports clothing, equipment and technology
- Planning and delivering warm-ups to participants.

There are three learning outcomes in this component.

A Explore types and provision of sport and physical activity for different types of participant
- A1 Types and providers of sport and physical activities
- A2 Types and needs of sport and physical activity participants
- A3 Barriers to participation in sport and physical activity for different types of participant
- A4 Methods to address barriers to participation in sport and physical activity for different types of participant

B Examine equipment and technology required for participants to use when taking part in sport and physical activity
- B1 Different types of sports clothing and equipment required for participation in sport and physical activity
- B2 Different types of technology and their benefits to improve sport and physical activity participation and performance
- B3 The limitations of using technology in sport and physical activity

C Be able to prepare participants to take part in sport and physical activity.
- C1 Planning a warm-up
- C2 Adapting a warm-up for different categories of participants and different types of physical activities
- C3 Delivering a warm-up to prepare participants for physical activity

Assessment

This unit is internally assessed. This means that your teacher will mark it. There are 3 tasks in the assessment. These tasks are based around a vocational context that will be provided by your teacher.

A1 Types of providers of sport and physical exercise

Types of sport

Do you know the difference between a sport and a game? A sport must:

- be competitive – that is, sport is played against someone where the aim is to win or beat them
- involve some physical effort
- have rules and regulations
- have a National Governing Body (NGB) – in football this is the FA (Football Association).

An activity like chess does not count as a sport because there is no physical effort when playing chess.

> **Intro**
>
> In pairs, write down as many different sports as you can think of.

> **Key Term**
>
> Resilience being able to overcome setbacks
>
> NGB every sport has a National Governing Body which oversees the rules

Benefits of taking part in sport

There are many benefits to taking part in sport or physical activity.

- **Improve fitness.** All sport involves exercise. Regular exercise improves fitness, which has many health benefits.
- **Meet new people.** Sport is played with and against other people. Many people who take part in sport enjoy the social aspect as much as the sport. Sport is a great way to meet new people who have a shared interest.
- **Leadership.** A team needs people who can organise the other players. This is an example of leadership. In really good teams, all players show leadership skills at times. Leadership skills are very important in normal life too. Sport is a good way for people to develop these skills.
- **Team work.** People need to work together when playing team sports. Often, the most successful team is the one that works together the best – not the one with the best players. Working together is one of the most important skills that people need in everyday life. Sport allows people to develop these skills.
- **Resilience and self confidence.** Things go wrong when playing sport. You might make a mistake, or your opponent might win a lucky point. It is important not to let this get you down so you can continue with the game. This is called resilience. Resilience is a very important skill for everyday life.
- **Self confidence.** In all sports, players need to be confident in their own skills. If they were not confident they would not try.

Rowing is a sport that needs excellent teamwork

Individual sports

Individual sports are where one person competes alone. They may compete against one other person, such as in singles tennis, or against many other people, such as in athletics.

Singles tennis

Athletics

Fencing

Team sports

Team sports are where two people or more are work together to beat another team. There are many examples of team sports. Some familiar ones are:

Volleyball

Hockey

Softball

Activity

1. Match each photograph to a benefit of sport.

a

b

c

2. Jinna is 23. Her parents recently passed away and she doesn't have any other family. She lives alone. She used to enjoy sport when she was a young girl. a) What sport would you recommend she takes up? b) Which benefits of that sport would benefit Jinna?

Outdoor activities

An **outdoor activity** includes things like:

- rock climbing
- high ropes
- white water rafting
- abseiling.

Intro

In pairs, write down as many different outdoor activities as you can think of.

These kind of activities:

- need some level of skill
- involve some adventure
- include a small amount of risk
- need safety equipment, to manage those risks
- they take place outside or in activity centres.

Benefits of outdoor activities

There are many benefits to taking part in outdoor activities.

- **Positive risk taking**. Outdoor activities are challenging. They include a small amount of risk. Taking small risks, and overcoming them, makes people feel good about themselves. It is also good practice for everyday life. We normally achieve the most when we challenge ourselves.

- **Meet new people**. Groups of people help and support each other during outdoor activities. This can lead to new friendships.

- **Learn new skills**. Most people have not tried these activities before. They need to learn new skills. They need to learn about new equipment. Learning new skills is important in our lives.

- **Self confidence**. People feel happy about themselves when they become better at something. This boosts self esteem.

> **self esteem** how someone feels about themselves

- **Reduce stress**. People can become stressed by their day-to-day lives. They might be worried about exams or work. Outdoor activities need someone's full attention. This means they can't think about anything that is worrying them. This reduces people's stress, which is very important for mental health.

- **Reduce screen time**. Many people spend too much time looking at their phone or computer. People can't check their phones when they are rock climbing! Outdoor activities give people a break from their phones or computers, which is good for them.

Activity

1. What are the names of the activities shown in the photos?

a

b

c

d

2. Niall is very sociable but works long hours in an office. He wants to get fit and build upper body strength but does not want to join a gym or lift weights at home.

a) Recommend two different outdoor activities for him.

b) Justify why those activities are suitable for him.

A1

Physical fitness activities

Physical fitness activities help people to keep fit. They can focus on:

- general fitness, by exercising the heart and lungs
- strength, by exercising muscles
- both fitness and strength.

Unlike sport, these activities are not competitive.

Unlike outdoor activities, they are not adventurous.

Intro

In pairs, write down as many different fitness activities as you can think of.

Some examples are:

- dance classes – e.g. Zumba, aerobics
- circuit training
- body conditioning
- spinning classes
- boxercise.

A spinning class

A dance class

Strength training

Aqua aerobics

Benefits of physical activities

There are many benefits to taking part in physical activities.

- **Meet new people.** Exercise classes are often run in groups, where people can make new friends.
- **Improve body composition.** Lots of people worry about their bodies. Regular exercise can help people lose weight and build muscle. This can help them look and feel better.
- **Improve physical health.** Regular exercise is really good for people's health. Physical fitness activities can make people healthier and fitter.

> composition what something is made of

- **Improve confidence.** As people get fitter and stronger they feel happier. They feel more confident about themselves. People also tend to feel good immediately after exercise.
- **Set fitness goals.** Exercise classes often happen at the same time each week. This helps people to plan exercise around their lives. When people exercise regularly, they can set themselves fitness goals, such as: I want to be able to dance non-stop for 10 minutes in 6 weeks' time.

Activity

1. List the benefits of physical activity that you think each photograph shows.

a
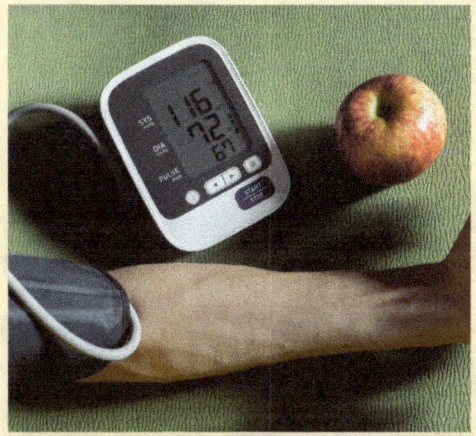

b

c

d

2. Sally is in her 80s and lives in sheltered housing. She is overweight and has trouble with her knee joints. a) Explain why aqua aerobics would be a good activity for her.
b) Explain why cycling is a less suitable activity for Sally.

Public sector provision

The **public sector** means all organisations that are run by or controlled by the government.

Organisations which are part of the public sector include:

- central government
- local authorities (also known as local councils)
- state schools
- Sports England

State schools

Schools must promote the physical development of students. That is why PE is compulsory at school.

As well as PE, schools also provide after-school sports clubs and enter teams into local leagues.

Intro

In pairs, write down as many different public sector organisations you can think of.

State schools often work with local authorities and use the same venues.

Local authorities

Local authorities invest a lot of money into sport facilities. These include local swimming pools and leisure centres.

Sport England

Sport England is a government body that develops grassroots sport and aims to get people active.

It provides funding and works with other public bodies. It also works with the voluntary and private sector.

Characteristics of the public sector

Funding

Public sector organisations are given money by the government. This money comes from

- taxes on people and businesses
- the National Lottery.

Aims

The public sector's aim is to:

- get more people taking part in sport
- make sure everyone is fit and healthy.

The public sector aims to spend the money it is given each year. It does **not** try to make a profit.

Quality of provision

The quality of public sector facilities can vary. Some are new and in good condition. Others are older and not as good.

Facilities can include things like:

- playing fields
- play parks and skate parks

This outdoor gym in a park is an example of public sector provision.

- leisure centres
- swimming pools
- outdoor bowling greens
- gyms
- ice rinks

Accessibility

The public sector aims to include everybody.

- Anyone can take part.
- Some groups may take part for free.

- For those that pay, the cost is relatively cheap.

The sector will try to attract groups who may not take part in sport and activity. For instance:

- running sessions for older people at the leisure centre

- encouraging all genders to take part in a full range of sports
- providing access to clubs and facilities for people who would otherwise not afford it.

	Advantages	Disadvantages
Types and range of provision	Common sports and activities covered	Minority sport and activities not often provided
Types and range of equipment	Equipment is cheaper or free to borrow or use	Less equipment and smaller range of different types of equipment Equipment more likely to be older, more basic – although not always
Cost of taking part	In some cases, provision or facilities might be free e.g. in schools, outdoor gyms for everyone to use If there is a cost, it is generally cheaper e.g. in public leisure centres There are often discounts for certain groups, e.g. pensioners, unemployed and young people	When there is a cost, people may still be excluded
Access to different types of sport and activities	Provides access to common sports and activities for a wide range of people	Fewer sports and activities on offer e.g. minority sports are unlikely to be offered
Additional services		Fewer or no additional services such as childcare or café

Activity

1. Write out the following sentences and fill in the missing words.

a) The public sector is funded by the g_____.

b) Public sector sports are f___ or cheaper than those in the private sector.

c) Local le___ centres and s_____ p___ are often run by the public sector.

2. Cleo is a single mum with two small children. She has two jobs in order to pay all her bills. She wants to take up a sport.

a) Recommend a sport for her that would be offered by the public sector.

b) i) Which advantages of public sector provision would benefit Cleo?

ii) Which disadvantages of public sector provision would be a drawback for Cleo?

Private sector provision

The **private sector** means companies owned by someone other than the government.

There are lots of private sector providers of sport. For example:

- private 5-aside football pitches
- private gyms such as Fitness First, Pure Gym and David Lloyd
- 'for profit' golf clubs.

> **Starter**
>
> With a partner, make a list of all the private sector companies you can think of.

The private sector also runs outdoor activity centres. For instance:

- PGL
- Go Ape.

Characteristics of the private sector

Funding

The private sector funds itself by making a profit on fees to take part. Some profits are spent on staff and facilities.

Profits allow private companies to continue to provide sport and exercise facilities.

Aims

Private companies' main aim is to make a profit. If they can't make a profit then they can't pay their bills and have to close.

Private companies may have other aims too.

- Some companies understand they have an impact on their community and the world. This is known as Corporate and Social Responsibility (CSR). They may have aims connected to their CSR.

Quality of provision

The facilities are normally very good. This is because the profits can help pay for newer equipment more often.

People paying higher prices expect facilities to be very good.

Good facilities mean:

- the equipment is new
- there is lots of equipment
- there are lots of members of staff
- there are extra services such as sports therapists, sports massages, saunas
- there are nice added extras, such a café, lots of showers, childcare for children etc.

Accessibility

The private sector is less accessible than public or voluntary provision.

The private sector needs to attract people who can afford to pay:

- They may target some groups of people more than others. This tends to leave out other groups, who may not feel welcome.
- The higher cost of private provision means some people cannot afford it.
- The amount of private provision also varies with location. For instance, there is much more private provision in cities than rural areas.

A modern private gym has lots of up-to-date equipment.

	Advantages	Disadvantages
Types and range of provision	Wide range of sports and activities	Minority sports are not covered as they are not profitable Provision is location-dependent – some areas may not have much private provision
Types and range of equipment	Wide range of equipment and large number of items of equipment Latest, most expensive models	There may be extra cost to hire or use speciality equipment
Cost of taking part	May provide discounts for certain groups e.g. students A higher cost means that more money can be spent on the latest equipment and employing highly-trained people	Can be expensive, which stops people taking part People might be excluded from sports or activities they might otherwise enjoy
Access to different types of sport and activities	Provides a wider range of sports and activities than the public sector	Only people with enough money can take part
Additional services	Access to additional services, such as childcare/creche, café/bar, sports therapist	

Activity

1. Are the following sentences true or false?

a) The private sector is normally more expensive than other sectors.

b) The private sector is funded by the local council.

c) The private sector only provides gyms.

d) Private sector equipment is normally very good.

e) All swimming pools are provided by the private sector.

f) The private sector provides sport facilities to the widest range of people.

2. Remind yourself about Cleo, the single mum in the last activity on the previous page.

a) Recommend a sport for her that would be offered by the private sector.

b) i) Which advantages of private sector provision would benefit Cleo?

ii) Which disadvantages of private sector provision would be a drawback for Cleo?

Voluntary sector provision

Voluntary organisations come in all shapes and sizes. They can be quite large clubs or small local groups who run on a tiny budget.

They are run:

- by volunteers who give up their time for free
- for the benefit of a community or group of people.

Like the public sector, they are not run to make a profit.

Intro

In one minute list as many voluntary local sports clubs as you can think of.

Unlike the public sector, the voluntary sector is separate from any government body.

Voluntary organisations can be things like:

- tennis clubs
- local amateur football clubs.
- Parkrun

Characteristics of the voluntary sector

Funding

Funding sources include:

- fundraising – for instance, asking people to raise money through sponsored events
- government – national or local government bodies may help with funding
- the National Lottery
- membership fees.

Aims

The voluntary sector does not aim to make a profit. However, it does need to make as much money as it spends.

Each organisation has specific aims. Typical aims of a voluntary sports organisation might include things like:

- to promote the sport or activity in the community
- to improve the health and well-being of participants
- to provide training with qualified coaches
- to ensure everyone receives equal treatment and equal opportunity to take part.

Quality of provision

There are such a wide range of voluntary organisations that quality of provision can vary.

Facilities

- A small local running club may have a small clubhouse but very few other facilities.
- A local sports club might offer a range of different sports and have a hall, bar, playing field and cafe.

Staff

People working in the voluntary sector do not get paid. For instance:

- the people who organise your local Parkrun do not get paid
- people coaching a local children's football club do not get paid.

These people give up their time because they are passionate about their sport or want to give something back to the local community.

A volunteer may not be as qualified as someone who earns their living through sport.

This volunteer coach may or may not have any formal coaching qualifications.

For instance:

- A volunteer who coaches children may not have any formal training.
- Whereas a coach who charges an hourly rate will have a range of qualifications and coaching badges.

However – some volunteers are well-qualified, and provide their services for free.

So, the quality of equipment and training does depend on the type and size of the organisation, and the people involved.

Accessibility

Voluntary organisations only charge fees to cover running costs. This means clubs can be very cheap to join. This means the voluntary sector is more accessible to a wider range of groups than the private sector.

The voluntary sector can also target people that the public sector misses.

Some voluntary organisations work with the public sector, to target people who would otherwise miss out.

	Advantages	Disadvantages
Types and range of provision	Wide range – minority provision more likely to be covered Responds to local demands	Provision still location-dependent
Types and range of equipment	Can focus on gaps in provision so may have equipment not available elsewhere	Smaller organisations unlikely to have the latest or best equipment
Cost of taking part	In some cases provision might be free Where there is a cost, people know that their money is not used to make a profit for anyone	There are normally some costs, even for very small organisations The lower costs mean the voluntary sector may not always be able to compete with private facilities
Access to different types of sport and activities	Provides access to a huge range of sports and activities Also provides access to a wide range of people	
Additional services		Normally fewer or no additional services – though there are exceptions

Activity

1. Explain what each of the terms in bold below mean.

a) The voluntary sector is **accessible** to lots of people.

b) The voluntary sector has a **wide range of facilities**.

c) The voluntary sector normally has fewer **facilities**.

2. Remind yourself about Cleo, the single mum on the previous pages. a) i) Recommend a sport for her that would be offered by the voluntary sector. ii) What are the advantages of voluntary sector provision of this sport? b) i) Which advantages of voluntary sector provision would benefit Cleo? ii) Which disadvantages of voluntary sector provision would be a drawback for Cleo?

A2 Types and needs of sport and physical activity participants

There are lots of different types of participant in sport and exercise. Everyone has different needs, and different reasons for taking part.

The UK government publishes recommendations for exercise. They recommend that different types of participants need:

- different amounts of exercise
- different types of exercise.

Intro
With a partner, try to work out how much exercise you do each week.

Age

We can break down ages into the following:

Primary school children (aged 5–11 years)
Adolescents (aged 12–17 years)

Moderate activity means you can talk but not sing.

Vigorous activity means it is difficult to talk.

Exercise
- across a week, an average of 60 minutes of moderate to vigorous activity per day
- these activities should be spread throughout the day
- activities should be varied, to promote muscle and bone strength
- minimise periods of inactivity

Disabled children and adolescents (5–17)

Exercise
- at least 20 minutes of moderate activity per day, broken into small chunks throughout the day
- even smaller amounts of physical activity are still good for you
- when starting from a low level of activity, build up slowly

Strength and balance
- challenging but manageable strength and balance activities 3 times a week

Adults (aged 18–49 years)

Exercise
- minimise periods of inactivity
- be physically active every day
- at least 150 minutes of moderate activity per week

OR
- 75 minutes of vigorous activity per week

OR
- a mixture of them both

Strength
- Strength-building exercises on at least two days per week. This could include weights, yoga, gardening or even carrying heavy bags.

Older adults (aged 50 years and up)

Exercise and strength:
- the same as younger adults, but building up slowly from their current levels

Balance and flexibility
- balance-improving activities twice per week, such as Tai Chi, bowls, or dancing

Additional needs

Participants may have:
- visual impairments
- hearing impairments
- physical impairments.

Participants may have long-term health conditions such as:
- asthma
- type 2 diabetes
- high blood pressure
- coronary heart disease (CHD).

> **asthma** a condition associated with breathing
> **diabetes** a condition associated with controlling the amount of sugar in the blood

However, the general recommended activity levels are the same for all adults. This is because there is little evidence that physical activity is unsafe for people with disabilities or health conditions, as long as people start with:
- low durations
- low intensities
- and build up over time as the body adjusts

Health needs

Physical activity and exercise can help with all kinds of health needs:

- physical health needs
- social health needs
- mental health needs.

Intro
Discuss how you feel after doing exercise.

Physical health

Activity and exercise has many benefits for physical health:

- improves fitness
- improves body composition – reduces fat mass and increases muscle mass
- it makes us tired so we sleep better
- improves the immune system, to help prevent illness,
- it helps prevent long-term health conditions, such as diabetes, heart disease and high blood pressure.

The Chief Medical Officers' Physical Activity Guidelines say:

"If physical activity were a drug, we would refer to it as a miracle cure, due to the great many illnesses it can prevent and help treat."

Social health needs

There are lots of social benefits to exercise too, such as:

- meeting new people and making new friends
- having fun
- developing leadership skills
- learning to work as part of a team.

All of these together help to decrease loneliness. This is very important because loneliness can have a big impact on mental health.

Mental health needs

Mental health is just as important as physical health. Physical activity also has benefits for mental health:

- decreases levels of stress and anxiety – sport and exercise can be an outlet for feelings of stress
- improves work-life balance – having interests outside of school or work is good for mental health
- improves mood – exercise releases chemicals in the brain that make us feel better
- increase self-confidence and self-esteem
- decreases the risk of depression

Activity

1. What additional exercise should older adults, aged 50+, do every week?
2. Which groups are not recommended to exercise?
3. Explain why physical exercise is good for mental health.
4. Carina is a 42-year-old woman. She is married with one small child who goes to nursery. Carina has a full-time job and works at home most days. She uses a laptop all day and works sitting down at the kitchen table. Carina has recently been diagnosed as diabetic.

Carina goes for a 20-minute walk every day and likes to do some gardening at the weekend.

a) Assess whether Carina is doing the recommended amount of exercise.

b) i) Give **two** examples of physical health benefits of exercise for Carina.

ii) Give **two** examples of social health benefits of exercise for Carina.

iii) Give **two** examples of mental health benefits of exercise for Carina.

A3 & A4 Barriers to participation and ways to remove barriers for different participants

Barriers to sport and physical activity participation

Despite all its health benefits, a large number of people do not do enough exercise.

There are lots of different reasons why people do not exercise. But sometimes there are barriers that stop them.

Cost of participation

Barrier 	Ways to address barrier 
Clothing and equipment ✗ People might not be able to afford specialist clothes and equipment needed to take part	✓ Clothes and equipment could be discounted or hired for free
Transport ✗ People might not be able to afford to get to and from the venue	✓ Free or discounted public transport, free parking at venue

Access to sport or physical activity

Barrier 	Ways to address barrier 
Location ✗ People might not be able to reach the venue easily	✓ Run special buses ✓ Cycle or e-scooter hire schemes ✓ Alternative venues
Accessibility problems ✗ Venue or transport is not accessible to people with impairments or disabilities	✓ Ramps and lifts at venue and on buses ✓ Assistive equipment such as pool hoists in a swimming pool ✓ Assistive aids such as hearing loops for hearing aids

Continued...

Barrier 	Ways to address barrier 
Accessibility problems (continued)	✓ Signs and information provided in Braille ✓ Staff training to make sure all people's needs are recognised and supported
Types of sport or activity ✗ Some people might be interested in sports or activities that are not offered	✓ Offer a wider range of sports and activities ✓ Find out what local people might be interested in

Lack of time

Barrier 	Ways to address barrier 
Lack of time ✗ People may have small children to look after ✗ People may have no free time during the day, due to school or work	✓ Include a creche (childcare) option ✓ Open early and close late so people at work or school can still attend

Personal barriers

Barrier 	Ways to address barrier 
Body image and lack of self-confidence ✗ Some people do not want to use public changing rooms ✗ Some do not want to wear sports clothes as they feel they are too tight or revealing	✓ Create private changing rooms ✓ Allow people to wear the clothes they feel most comfortable in ✓ Use a wide range of different body types in images for advertising and marketing material
Influence of parent or guardian ✗ If parent or guardian is not interested in sports or activity then this can stop young people going	✓ Offer family sessions, or parent and child activities, to encourage a family-friendly culture
Fitness, health and participation ✗ May be unfit ✗ May be a long time since last did any physical activity or sport ✗ May never have done sport or activities ✗ May worry that exercise is bad for an existing health condition ✗ Pregnant women may worry that exercise is bad for them or their baby	✓ Run campaigns aimed at different groups to show that physical activity benefits everyone ✓ Run sessions that focus on these groups or individuals. E.g. the 'couch to 5k' programme is a good example of such a campaign. ✓ Make sure staff have the right training to run sessions for all conditions

Cultural barriers

Barrier 	Ways to address barrier 
Gender ✗ Some people are not comfortable taking part when genders are mixed	✓ Run sessions catering for different genders, such as women-only swimming
Clothing ✗ Sports clothing might be inappropriate for some people due to cultural reasons	✓ Make sure appropriate alternative clothing is available ✓ Make sure staff are trained in cultural awareness and are flexible regarding clothing
Role models ✗ A lack of role models from someone's own cultural background can make people feel the activity is not for them	✓ A diverse workforce can make people from a range of different backgrounds feel welcome

Activity

1. Fariq is a 27 year old man who lives with his girlfriend. They have just bought a new house which means most of his money is spent on bills and things for the house. He enjoyed tennis at school but none of his friends did. His family do not take part in physical activities or sport. He doesn't have a car and his nearest leisure centre is 5 miles away.

a) Describe the barriers to Fariq's participation in sport and physical activity.

b) Describe how each of these barriers could be overcome.

2. Sally is a retired doctor on a comfortable pension. She looks after her grandchildren three days a weeks. She used to go swimming but she felt self-conscious in her swimming costume. She stopped swimming after being diagnosed with high blood pressure.

a) Describe the barriers to Sally's participation in sport and physical activity.

b) Describe how each of these barriers could be overcome.

B1 Different types of sports clothing and equipment for participation

Lots of different clothing and equipment is used in sport and physical activities.

> **Intro**
>
> With a partner, write down the sports clothes that you have used in PE at school.

Clothing

Sports clothing performs a number of different roles. Clothes for each sport or activity are chosen for a range of reasons.

Body temperature

Shorts and a vest or T-shirt are often worn to expose the legs and arms. This keeps people cool, as exercise makes people warm.

However some sports in cold conditions need the arms and legs covered. For example:

- wetsuits used in triathlons and windsurfing
- body suits used in skiing

Weather

Waterproof layers might be needed in very wet conditions.

For example, a waterproof running jacket.

Protection

In some sports, clothing provides some level of protection, such as:

- a motor-racing suit for protection from fire
- padded shorts for cycling
- gloves for goalkeepers
- thick socks for rugby and football.

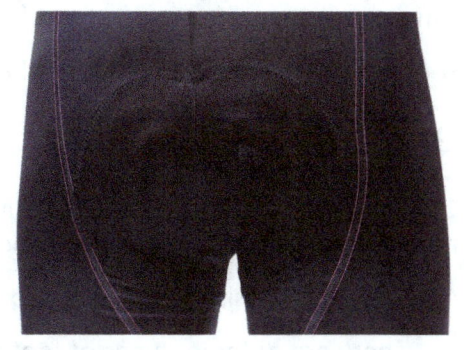

Performance

Clothes are also chosen to help with performance. This includes:

- allowing a full range of movement – not being tight and restrictive
- helping minimise drag, for instance when cycling fast
- it takes less effort to move in lightweight clothes – this can make a big difference over a long tennis match or an ultra-marathon.

Recovery

Compression clothing is now widely used in a number of sports. This tight-fitting layer helps with recovery because it reduces muscle vibrations, swelling and muscle soreness.

There are claims that compression clothing also helps with performance during sport or activity. However the evidence for that is mixed.

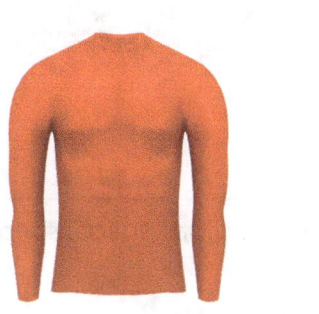
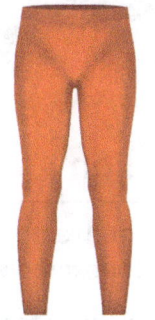

Training

- Leggings keep people warm when resting.
- Bibs are used during competitive practice.

Activity

1. List the different types of clothing for the following:
   - basketball
   - volleyball
   - yoga
   - mountain biking

2. For each of your answers describe why each piece of clothing is worn in each activity.

Footwear

Different footwear is needed for different sports and activities.

Footwear is chosen for a number of different reasons.

Intro

With a partner, think of three sports with different footwear.

Grip

Certain sports take place on different surfaces. Specific footwear is used for each surface and sport:

- Different tennis shoes for clay, grass and hard courts.
- There are different types of football boots for firm grass, soft grass, astroturf, 3G and 4G pitches. Each has different types of studs or blades.
- Running spikes should only be used on synthetic tracks.
- There are different running trainers for road and off-road running.
- There are a range of different cricket shoes for different roles in the game e.g. fast bowler versus all-rounder.
- Trainers used for indoor surfaces e.g. basketball and badminton.

Function

Some footwear forms part of the specialist equipment used for the sport, for example:

- clip shoes for cycling
- ice-skating and ice-hockey boots.

Protection

All footwear provides protection for the foot and ankle. For example:

- ankle support for sports with changes of direction, e.g. tennis, basketball, rugby
- protection for the toes when kicking a football
- protection for the toes for fast bowlers coming to a stop
- shock absorption and cushioning for sports with quick, sudden movements e.g. netball, squash.

Performance

Lightweight shoes or boots give a performance boost. This is because it is easier to accelerate, and run for a long time, in lightweight shoes.

Modern running trainers have a certain amount of 'springiness' – this helps people to run more efficiently.

Activity

1. List the different types of footwear for the following sports:
   - rugby
   - netball
   - ice-hockey
   - skiing
   - trail running
   - bouldering
   - 5-aside football on a 3G pitch
2. For each of your answers explain why each item is worn in each activity.

Sport-specific equipment

Most sports require some equipment.

Participation equipment

Some equipment is needed in order to take part. Examples include:

- balls and similar – tennis ball, golf ball, squash ball, shuttlecock
- rackets, clubs and bats
- javelin, pole vault, discuss.

> **Intro**
>
> In 1 minute, write down all the sport equipment your school has.

Travel-related equipment

In some travelling sports you need special items in order to take part. For example:

- a bicycle in cycling events
- a kayak, canoe or boat in rowing and related events
- a skateboard in boarding.

Scoring equipment

Equipment is used as part of the scoring process in some sports:

- goalposts in football, rugby, hockey and lacrosse
- nets in tennis, badminton, padel
- targets in archery
- bases in softball.

Fitness equipment

Lots of different equipment can be used for fitness training, such as:

- yoga mats
- dumbbells, barbells and kettlebells
- exercise balls.

Protection and safety equipment

Safety and protective equipment is very important:

Mouth protection

Mouth guards (gum shields) are used in sports such as rugby, hockey and American football, to protect the teeth and gums.

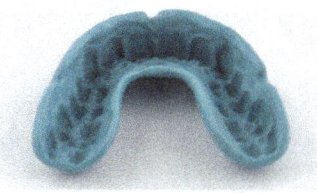

Head protection

Helmets are used in many sports including cycling, ice hockey, American football, cricket and fencing.

Head guards are used in amateur boxing and can be used in rugby and football.

Eye protection

The eyes are at particular risk during many sports.

- Goggles are used in sports such as cycling, skiing and squash.
- Sunglasses provide protection from harmful ultraviolet light for performers outside in summer – particularly for sports such as cricket, baseball and sailing.

A serious injury can lead to permanent damage to sight or even blindness. The National Eye Institute in the United States defines the following sports as high risk for eye injury: baseball, basketball, watersports, boxing, hockey, paintball, racketball, softball, squash, fencing, lacrosse and wrestling.

Although not widely adopted, goggles or safety glasses should be considered for these and other sports.

Body protection

Body protection reduces the effects of impacts. It is used in sports such as American football, mountain biking, fencing, cricket, baseball and ice hockey.

Flotation devices

Flotation devices are used in watersports, such as sailing and paddle-boarding, in case someone falls in the water. They help people remain above the water level.

First aid equipment

Injuries will occur during sport and activity. First aid kits include essential items such as:

- ice packs – to reduce swelling for sprains and strains
- bandages – to provide compression, and to apply to wounds
- defibrillator – used in an emergency for people who have had a heart – it applies an electric current to restart the heart.

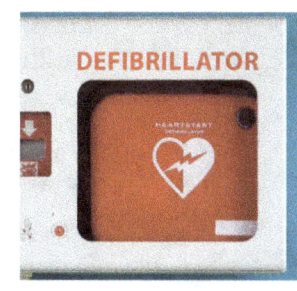

Equipment and assistive technology for people with disabilities

Equipment and technology can be used to ensure access for people with disabilities.

- 5-aside football for people with visual impairments – the ball has a bell inside which allows people to hear where it is

- Goalball is a Paralympic sport for people with visual impairments. It also includes a bell inside the ball.

- Running blades for high-performance running.

- Adapted table-tennis tables that have enough room between the end of the table and the table leg for wheelchairs to fit underneath.

- Wheelchairs adapted for speed or manoeuvrability, for example:

    * wheelchairs adapted for racing are as light as possible, and have three angled wheels to aid stability

    * wheelchairs adapted for basketball have a backrest and extra small wheels at the back, so the competitor can lean back without tipping over

    * adaptations are also used in wheelchair badminton, tennis and rugby.

- Gloves are an important piece of equipment for people using wheelchairs.

- Bicycle handlebars can be adapted for people with arm impairments.

- Handcycles are used by people with leg impairments.

- In para ice-hockey, competitors use a specially designed sledge

- Mono-skis are used for people with leg impairments.

- Weight-lifting hooks and harnesses that allow people with limb impairments to lift free weights.

- Additions to existing gym equipment can make it accessible for people with disabilities – for example, extra handles at the right height for wheelchair users.

- Gym equipment with high contrast (e.g. black and white) can benefit some visually impaired participants.

- Treadmills can be adapted for wheelchair use.

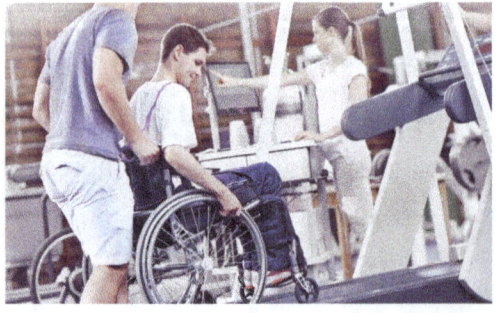

Facilities

There are lots of different facilities for sports and activities.

Indoor facilities

These include:

- sports halls, which are used for sports such as badminton, basketball and volleyball
- fitness gyms often have a range of different rooms, including dance and yoga studios
- indoor swimming pools, which often include a separate small pool for children
- velodromes
- climbing wall.

Outdoor facilities

These include:

- outdoor pitches – these can be grass or synthetic, full-size or smaller
- artificial snow domes
- running track
- tennis courts
- cycle tracks.

> **Intro**
>
> In 1 minute write down all the sport facilities in your school.

> synthetic made by people, not natural

> **Activity**
>
> 1. a) List all the equipment and facilities needed to take part in:
>   - triathlons
>   - wheelchair basketball
>   - handball
>   - ice-skating
>   - boccia
>   - weight training
>
>   b) Categorise each of your answers above as: clothing, footwear, sport-specific, protective equipment, facilities.

Officiating equipment

Equipment is needed to allow officials to run and control matches and events.

At an amateur level, the most common equipment is:

- whistle
- flag.

At an elite level, officials use microphones and earpieces to communicate with each other, and with the supporters or audience.

Intro

Can you think of any equipment used by officials that is not listed here?

Performance analysis

Performance analysis is increasingly useful for performers at any level. All sorts of data are captured about an athlete's performance.

Even for amateur performers, there is lots of useful technology:

- GPS watches – used by runners, cyclists and swimmers to track their location and distance
- heart rate monitors – either chest straps or wrist monitors that track the number of heartbeats per minute
- apps – used on smartphones and tablets to connect to GPS watches and heart rate monitors
- smart watches – these also run apps and can combine the functions of smartphones, GPS watches and heart rate monitors.

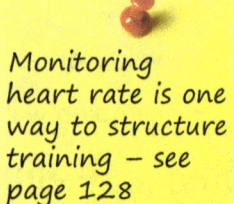

Monitoring heart rate is one way to structure training – see page 128

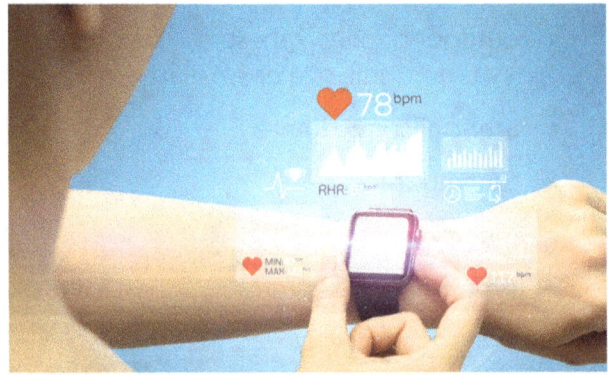

Activity

1. a) List the equipment used by officials in:
   - tennis
   - field hockey
   - cricket
   - track athletics

   b) Describe what each piece of equipment is used for in each case.

2. Explain how an amateur runner could use performance analysis equipment to improve their running times.

3. Ellisa is 18 and has just started a new course at her local FE college. The college has a good sport department, and Ellisa is determined to try out a new sport. She decides to join the women's rugby team. She is excited but a bit nervous about getting injured.

   a) Explain all the equipment she will need to take part. Remember to justify why she needs each piece of equipment.

   b) Describe the facilities her college will need to have for her to play and train.

B2 Technology benefits to improve participation and performance

Technology brings many benefits to sport and physical activity.

Clothing and footwear

Technology has had a big impact on sports clothing and footwear.

Changes in design, materials and manufacturing have led to better performances by athletes.

Thermoregulation

'Wicking' fabrics draw sweat from the skin to the outer layer of the fabric. These fabrics are also quick to dry. This helps performers keep cool, and also stops the clothes from getting heavy with sweat.

MOISTURE WICKING

Aerodynamics

In speed sports, clothing design and materials can reduce wind resistance (drag). This produces a performance benefit in sports such as:

- speed skating
- cycling
- ski jumping
- sprinting.

The same idea applies to water sports, through the use of swimming costumes and caps.

Footwear

Modern sport shoes have complex designs and are made of sophisticated materials.

Their main aims are:

- to be as light as possible whilst still providing cushioning, support and protection for the sport
- to provide high levels of grip, as needed for the sport and surface
- to aid running form and efficiency.

Modern running trainers are designed to have a certain amount of **rebound**. Rebound is when the energy from placing the foot down is stored. This helps to launch the foot during the next step.

For the best rebound, the latest designs use large foam soles and contain curved carbon plates. The plates are stiff and are proven to increase running efficiency, resulting in faster times.

Sport-specific equipment

Technology impacts the way that sport equipment is made. It impacts in two main ways:

- the development of new materials
- new design and engineering ideas.

Most updates are a combination of both.

Intro

Can you name the material that footballs used to be made of?

composite: something made of two separate materials

New materials

New materials continue to be developed by scientists. Engineers who make sports equipment are looking for materials that are light yet strong.

Materials that combine these two things are used to make modern sports equipment.

Tennis rackets

- Originally frames were made from wood…
- …but these were replaced with aluminium frames….
- …which were then replaced by modern graphite frames. This is because graphite is lighter and stronger than aluminium.
- As a result, modern tennis rackets can generate more power than older rackets – meaning that serves and other strokes are more powerful.

Racing bikes

Modern racing bikes are made of exotic materials such as carbon fibre.

- Carbon fibre is an example of a **composite**. A composite is a mixture of two or more separate materials.
- Modern composite materials are very light and strong. Carbon fibre is five times stronger than steel but much lighter.
- A carbon-fibre racing bike is very light, which means it takes less effort to ride fast. This benefits performance.

Formula 1 racing cars are also made of carbon fibre.

New designs

Equipment is constantly redesigned to increase performance.

The sport that probably spends the most time and money redesigning equipment is Formula 1 motor racing. Each year, every team is allowed to spend $135 million dollars. There are currently ten teams – so that's $1.35 billion dollars spent each year, to try and find improvements in performance.

Another example of equipment redesign is the golf driver:

- These clubs used to be made of wood and had a small head.
- New materials were introduced – first steel, then titanium, both lighter and stronger than wood.
- To increase performance to take advantage of the new materials, the head of the club was redesigned and enlarged

Modern pro golfers use these clubs to hit the golf ball much further than was possible in the past – so much so that golf courses had to be made larger!

Activity

1. a) i) What technologies are used in professional road cycling clothing?
   ii) Describe the benefits to cycling performance of each technology.

2. a) i) How has technology affected the design of tennis shoes in the last 40 years?
   ii) Describe the impact of each technology.

3. a) Explain how the design and materials of footballs have changed in the last 50 years.
   b) What impacts have these changes had on i) participation, ii) performance?

4. Describe which aspects of performance are most important when designing a hockey stick.

5. Yuen wants to join a gym to train her muscular endurance and aerobic endurance. List four different ways in which technology might impact participation in a gym.

6. Brian is in his 70s and has just completed his 50th marathon. However, he has not bought any new running gear for years.

Recommend some new clothing, footwear and equipment for Brian. Justify how and why each choice will benefit Brian.

Protection and safety equipment

Advances in technology can make some sports potentially more dangerous – for instance, racing at higher speeds.

However technology has also led to improvements in protection and safety equipment.

There are two types of improvements:

- improved protection
- improved performance.

> **Intro**
>
> Which parts of the body benefit most from safety equipment?

Improved protection

New materials and designs make equipment safer. For example:

- Cricket helmets offer greater protection than in the past. This is possible because of stronger, lighter materials, that can withstand the impact of very fast balls.
- Shin pads were made of leather in nineteenth century. Modern shin pads are far more effective. They use a mixture of materials, including composites. Because they are lighter, they are less intrusive for the player.
- Headgear in rugby needs to be soft to protect all players. The designs are developed to offer better protection from collisions whilst not posing a danger to other players.

Improved performance

New materials and designs can also improve the performance of safety equipment.

Track cycling helmets are a good example of an improved design aiding performance.

- These helmets are more aerodynamic, creating less drag, which aids performance.
- However, they are still as safe and offer as much protection.

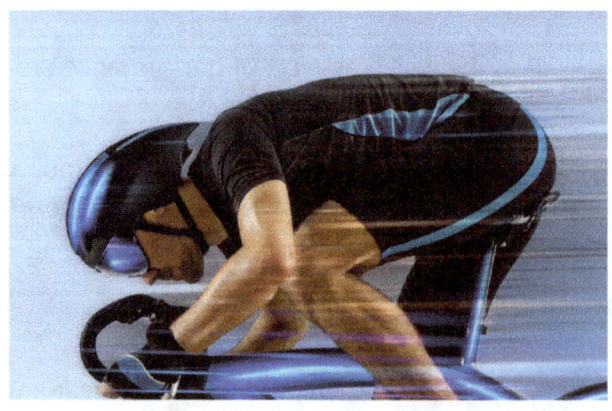

Equipment and assistive technology for people with disabilities

Technology has created better equipment and technology for people with disabilities.

Prosthetic limbs

- A prosthetic limb is an artificial limb. It is designed to replace some of the function of the missing limb.
- Modern prosthetic limbs are strong yet light. They are made of advanced materials, such as carbon fibre.
- Prosthetics allow people to take part in a wider range of sports or activities. They remove some barriers that might stop people with disabilities from taking part in physical activity.

Sports adaptations

Sports wheelchairs use improved designs and materials:

- Racing wheelchairs are made of lightweight materials, to improve performance in races.
- The three-wheel design is faster and far more manoeuvrable than standard wheelchairs.
- Angled rear wheels make sure the chair does not tip over when going around corners.

Assistive technologies

- Hearing loops make gyms and sports facilities more accessible to people with hearing impairments.
- The use of special raised tape allows a person with visual impairments to feel where they are on a court.
- Wireless microphones and receivers worn by coaches and referees can help people with hearing impairments.
- Modern buildings are designed to be accessible, with no-step access. Older buildings can include special lifts to make spaces accessible.
- Gyms and leisure centres have websites that are accessible for people with visual impairments.
- Smartphone apps are able to translate text into audio and translate spoken words into text. These can be used in training, coaching and competitions.

Activity

Akeyo is a wheelchair user. She wants to attend her local leisure centre.

1. Describe the technology the leisure centre could put in place to help Akeyo.

2. Akeyo wants to take part in wheelchair basketball. a) What clothing and equipment would you recommend for her? b) What technology is used in each suggestion and how would the technology benefit Akeyo?

Facilities

Simulation

Some equipment can **simulate** a real environment. (Simulate means 'to imitate'.)

- Treadmills allow runners to train indoors. Some provide settings that can recreate hills, which is a good form of training.

- Cyclists can use computers to help them train. Special computer software simulates different routes and terrain. Cyclists can even compete with other riders online. The equipment measures lots of performance data, including their speed and power.

- Motor racing uses very sophisticated simulators, so that drivers can learn about new circuits and cars.

Playing surfaces

Technology has developed new artificial surfaces. They are used in lots of sports but particularly football and tennis. Examples include:

- 3G and 4G football pitches
- acrylic tennis courts
- synthetic running tracks.

They have two main benefits:

- **They are all-weather surfaces**. They are designed so water easily drains away. In contrast, grass pitches or concrete courts can take a long time to dry out.

- **They reduce the risk of injury**. For example, 4G football surfaces are much safer to play football on than concrete 5-aside pitches. They are also safer than poor-quality grass pitches, as bumps and holes can cause injury.

Intro

List the different surfaces have you played sports on.

Other surfaces also reduce the risk of injury:

- A sprung floor is used in dance studios and gyms. It has a small amount of give, which softens impacts from landings or falls.

- Mats are also used to cushion landings and prevent injuries.

Officiating

Technology has become an important tool for officials in top-level sport

Computer-assisted systems

Computer technology is used in a number of sports:

- Cricket – the Decision Review System tracks the movement of the ball and predicts where it would have gone. This is useful for LBW decisions.
- Tennis – Hawk-Eye tracks the movement of the ball and can check if part of the ball touched a line.
- Football – goal-line technology checks if all the ball went behind the line in order to count as a goal.
- Athletics – starter blocks are monitored by computers to check for false starts.

These systems are very accurate. They help stop incorrect decisions such as good serves being called out and goals not being given.

Video-assisted decision making

Video replays, from multiple angles, are used in a number of sports to help officials make decisions about incidents. Common examples are:

- Video Assistant Referee (VAR) in football
- Decision Review System (DRS) in cricket
- Television Match Official (TMO) in rugby union
- Video Referee in rugby league
- Instant Replay Process in American football (NFL)

The benefits of these systems are that:

- They can review incidents that the on-field officials miss.
- They provide a number of different angles of an incident, that on-field officials cannot see.
- They help to ensure the rules of the game are followed.

> **Activity**
>
> 1. Benson wants to train for 11-aside football on Sundays by playing 5-aside football, once per week, in the evening. There are two local clubs – one plays on grass, the other on a 3G synthetic pitch. Evaluate the benefits and limitations of each playing surface for Benson.
>
> 2. Goran is a 40 year old amateur runner. Describe the different ways in which technology could help Goran in his training.

Performance analysis

Technology is used in training and competition to capture data about the performance.

- **Action cameras.** These are used to record a performer.

  * They can show what happened in the heat of competition.

  * Or, they can be used to capture slow-motion footage, to help improve technique. High-speed cameras can capture lots of detail. For example, gait analysis cameras are used to help performers choose the right running shoes.

> gait the way someone walks and runs

- **GPS** allows users to track their position accurately. This provides lots of data about how far someone ran or cycled, at what pace, and for how long. This can help with both tactics and fitness.

  * For example, a tennis player might waste too much energy early in a match. Or a rugby player might need to work on increasing her acceleration rate.

- **Sensors on clothing or equipment.** These can provide all sorts of information about health or performance. Modern top-level sport uses lots of sensor data to improve players' performance and fitness.

- **Software applications** can be used with all of the above, to further analyse and make sense of data. They can present it in a form that is easily understandable.

All of these technologies can help the individual or team to measure and improve fitness, tactics or techniques.

B3 The limitations of using technology in sport and physical activity

Despite all its benefits, technology also has some disadvantages.

Time

There may be a time cost to use technology. For example:

It may take time to set up:

- Systems such as Hawk-Eye in tennis take time to set up accurately on each court

It may take time to use the equipment:

- For instance, it takes time to learn how to play with a new badminton racket made from a different material.
- It can take a lot of time to use video assisted decision-making, which interrupts the flow of the game.

It takes time to pull together data and give good feedback to the participant:

- Professional sports collect a large amount of performance analysis data. Someone has to go through that data, make sense of it and use it to give meaningful feedback.

> **Intro**
> Explain what you think is meant by 'time cost'.

Cost of technology

There is an initial cost and a running cost associated with most technology:

- They latest clothing and footwear technology is expensive.
- Hi-tech equipment is very expensive – for example racing bikes and racing wheelchairs. Repairs are also costly.
- The latest protective and safety equipment can be expensive and might need replacing regularly.
- Artificial playing surfaces are expensive to install – though running costs can be low.
- Simulation equipment has a high up-front cost, and in some cases there is an on-going subscription.
- Computer-assisted systems and video-assistant systems are very expensive to install and have on-going running costs.

- Performance analysis equipment can be very costly. At an elite level, there is also an on-going cost for a qualified person to interpret the data. However, some examples, notably GPS and phone apps, can be quite cheap and without running costs.

Access to technology

Because of the costs, a big problem with technology is equality of access.

This can result in unfair advantages for those who can afford it. For example:

- The best running shoes and racing bikes give users a small performance advantages.

- Not all athletes with disabilities have access to the same level of equipment – for example running blades for amateurs cost at least £2000. For professionals, that figure can rise to £20,000.

- Not everyone can afford to join a gym or club with the best facilities. Nor can everyone afford sophisticated simulation equipment.

- Only the big leagues or competitions in each sport can afford all of the latest officiating technology.

- Performance analysis equipment helps improve performance. However, the high costs mean that, for example, only the big football clubs can afford all the equipment. This widens the performance gap between them and less wealthy football clubs.

Accuracy of data

It is common to assume that technology is always right. However, this is not the case.

Computer assisted systems to help officials are not 100% accurate. For example:

- Systems that judge whether balls have crossed a line are often accurate to within a few millimetres. This is called a margin of error, and is quite normal. But that means it can be wrong if the ball is a few millimetres inside or outside the line.

Performance analysis data is not always accurate. For example:

- GPS measurements have a margin of error. If you use GPS data to judge pace, it can mean you are running too fast or slow.

- Heart-rate monitors and other sensors also have a margin of error. This means that it can sometimes be better to use 'perceived exertion' rather than heart rate for training.

margin of error how accurate a measurement is

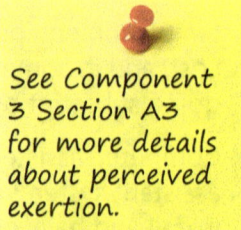

See Component 3 Section A3 for more details about perceived exertion.

Usability

Usability is an important consideration for using technology. For example:

- A tennis racket that can generate the most power, but is very hard to control, is not very usable.
- Participants might need training to use new equipment – or might need to change technique.
- Sport-specific equipment for people with disabilities might be quite different from equipment they normally use. It might take them some time to get used to it.
- It can take time to get used to playing on new artificial surfaces.
- There have been problems in getting systems such as VAR to work so that fans, players and managers are happy.
- Performance analysis data and tools might be hard to understand or use. If that is the case then the data is not helpful because it can't be used to improve performance.
- In each case, extra training might be needed to make the best use of technology.

Activity

1. Your local handball team has hired a new coach. Explain how the coach could use performance analysis technology to improve the team.

2. State two limitations to using the latest carbon-fibre racing bikes.

3. Give three examples of time costs when using technology.

4. Your school is considering filming the inter-form football tournament. One teacher would be a video assistant referee, and look at footage as the games are played. Assess the benefits and limitations that this would bring to the tournament.

Mo is 35 and runs her own business. She is considering taking up squash at her local private sports club. She used to play sport in her early 20s but kept spraining her ankle. She does not know how fit she is now and is a bit worried that squash is quite intense. Mo has had a hearing impairment from birth.

5. a) i) Describe the items of clothing and footwear you would recommend to Mo. ii) Justify why you recommended each of them.

b) i) Describe the sporting equipment that Mo will need to play squash. ii) Give an example of an item of safety equipment that you would recommend, and explain why you recommended it.

c) What facilities should the sports club provide for Mo to play squash?

d) The squash team at the club takes part in a local league, with an umpire. What equipment would the umpire need?

e) Describe the types of technology that you would recommend for Mo. Remember that some of the technology might be associated with your answers to parts a), b) and c).

f) For each of your answers to part e) evaluate the benefits and limitations of Mo using that technology to play squash.

C1 Planning a warm-up

Before beginning any physical activity you must warm up. A warm-up lowers the risk of injury.

There are three parts to a warm-up:
- pulse-raiser
- mobiliser
- preparation stretches

> **Intro**
> Describe your normal warm-up.

intensity how hard exercise feels

Pulse-raiser

The first part of a warm-up is the **pulse-raiser**. These are activities that increase heart rate.

Pulse-raiser activities should gradually increase in *intensity*.

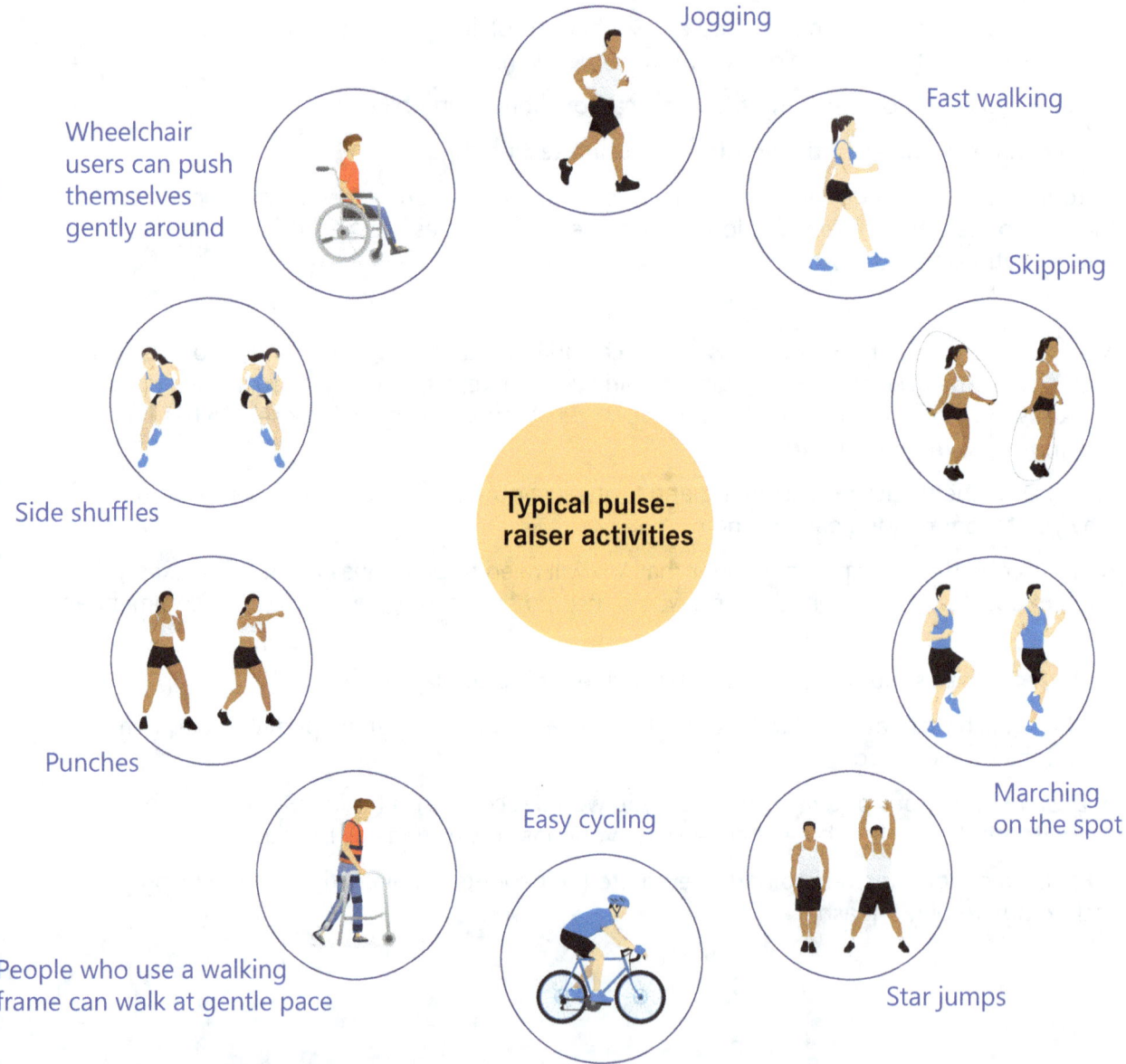

But any activity which raises heart rate and breathing rate is suitable as long as it starts gently and slowly increases in intensity.

Response of cardio-respiratory system to pulse-raiser

The cardio-respiratory system is made up of:

- the heart, blood vessels and blood
- the lungs, mouth, nose, windpipe and other air passages.

> **cardio** relating to the heart
> **respiratory** relating to breathing

These all work together to:

- breathe in oxygen,
- transfer oxygen into the bloodstream
- deliver oxygen in the blood to muscles around the body.

The two systems also remove carbon dioxide from muscles, transfer it into the bloodstream, and send it to the lungs where it is breathed out.

Effect of pulse-raiser exercises

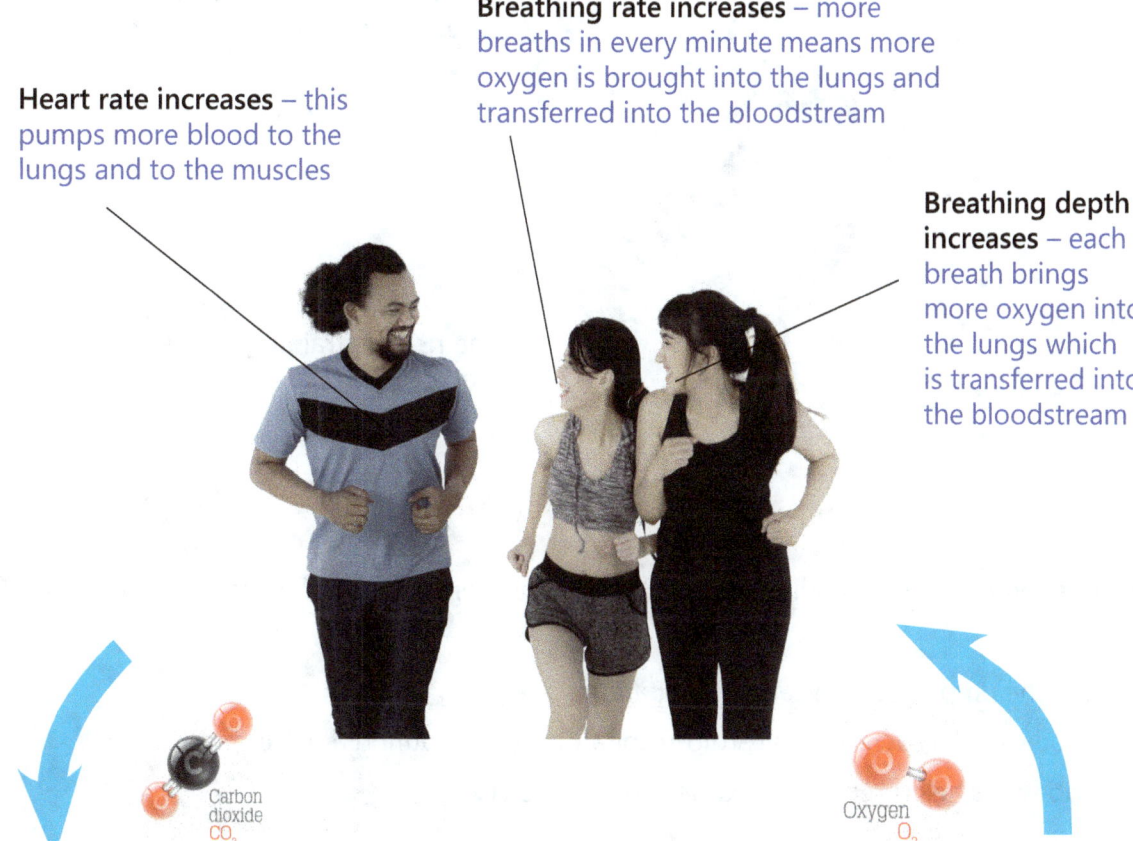

Heart rate increases – this pumps more blood to the lungs and to the muscles

Breathing rate increases – more breaths in every minute means more oxygen is brought into the lungs and transferred into the bloodstream

Breathing depth increases – each breath brings more oxygen into the lungs which is transferred into the bloodstream

More carbon dioxide is removed from the body – because the increased blood flow, breathing rate and breathing depth can remove the extra waste produced by muscles

All of this means there is more blood reaching the working muscles, and **more oxygen is being supplied** to them

Response of musculoskeletal system to pulse-raiser

The musculo-skeletal system is made up of:

- the muscles and tendons
- the skeleton and ligaments.

tendons connect muscles to bones

ligaments connect bones to other bones

These all work together to enable us to move.

Effect of pulse-raiser exercises

Muscle temperature increases as the muscles begin to work harder

As muscles warm up they **become more pliable** – this means they become more flexible

As they become more pliable, the **risk of straining a muscle decreases**

Activity

1. a) State the purpose of a pulse-raiser. b) List three different types of pulse-raiser activities.

2. a) State the purpose of the cardio-respiratory system.
   b) Describe what happens to the cardio-respiratory system during a pulse-raiser.
   c) How does this help prepare the participant for exercise?

3. Why is it important for pulse-raisers to begin gently and gradually increase in intensity?

4. a) State the purpose of the musculoskeletal system.
   b) Describe what happens to the musculoskeletal system during a pulse-raiser.
   c) How does this help prepare the participant for exercise?

Mobiliser

The second part of a warm-up is the **mobiliser**.

These are activities that move joints through their full range of movement.

They encourage the production of synovial fluid in the joints. Synovial fluids lubricates the joints so they can move smoothly and freely.

Mobiliser exercises should::

- start with small movements
- gradually and gently increase the range of movement.

Mobiliser exercises should always be smooth motions.

Intro

Can you think of any equipment used by officials that is not listed here?

synovial fluid a substance in the joints between moving bones

lubricate make something slippy

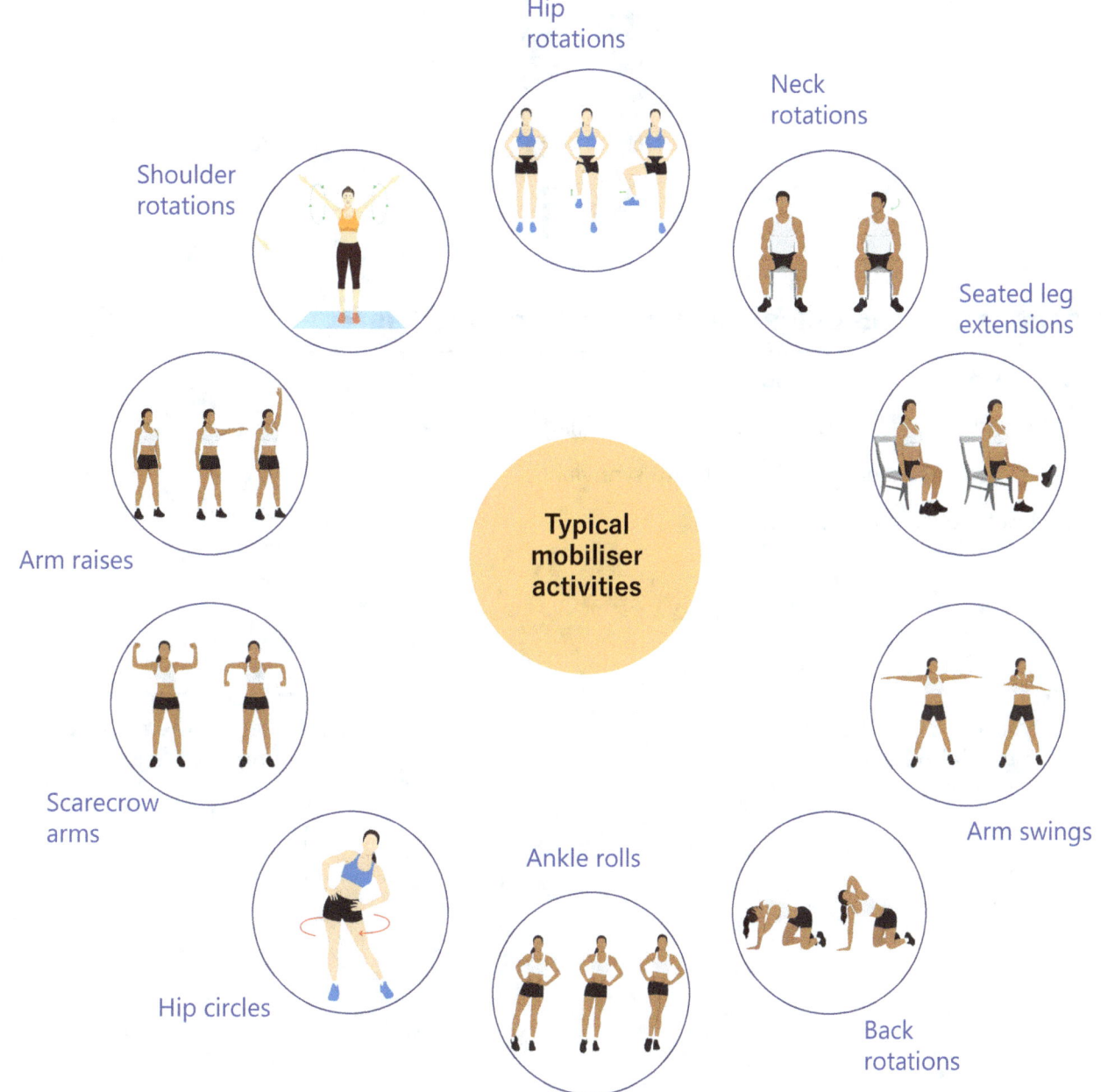

Typical mobiliser activities: Hip rotations, Neck rotations, Seated leg extensions, Arm swings, Back rotations, Ankle rolls, Hip circles, Scarecrow arms, Arm raises, Shoulder rotations

Response of cardio-respiratory system to mobiliser

Mobiliser exercises are less intense than pulse-raisers.

This has the following effect:

Slight drop in heart rate as exercise intensity drops

Slight drop in breathing rate as exercise intensity drops

Response of musculoskeletal system to mobiliser

A synovial joint is where two bones meet.
- The ends of the bones are covered with cartilage.
- The space between them is filled with synovial fluid.

This allows movement in the joint.

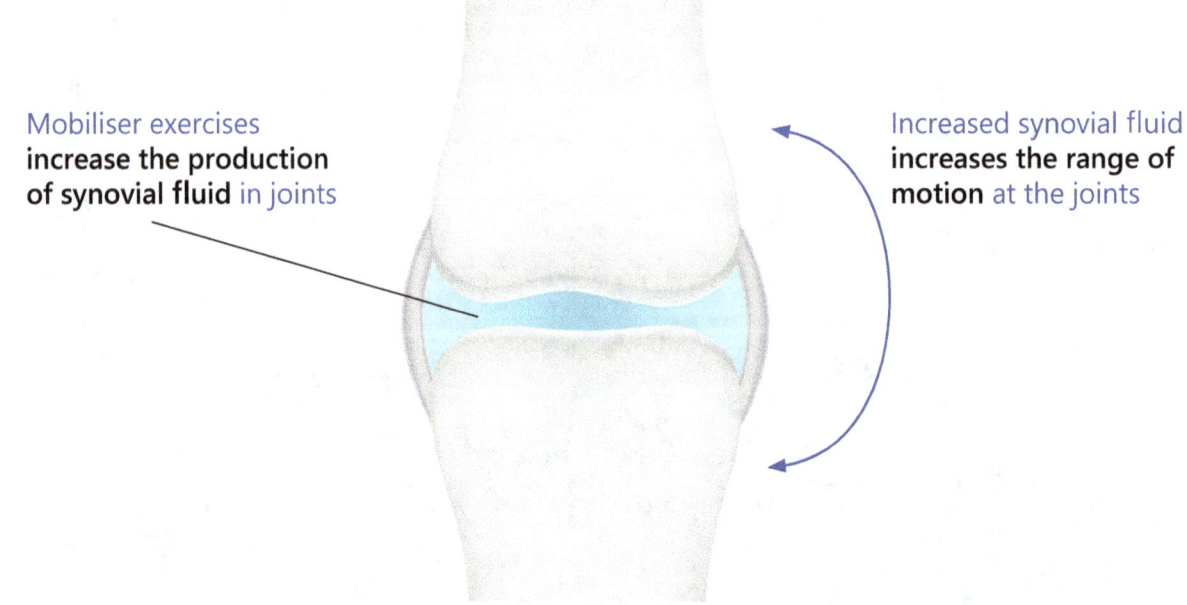

Mobiliser exercises **increase the production of synovial fluid** in joints

Increased synovial fluid **increases the range of motion** at the joints

Preparation stretch

The final part of a warm-up is the **preparation stretch**.

These stretches prepare muscles for more intense exercise.

Before learning about different preparation stretches, we need to know about the main muscle groups in the body.

> **Intro**
>
> Can you name any muscles in your body?

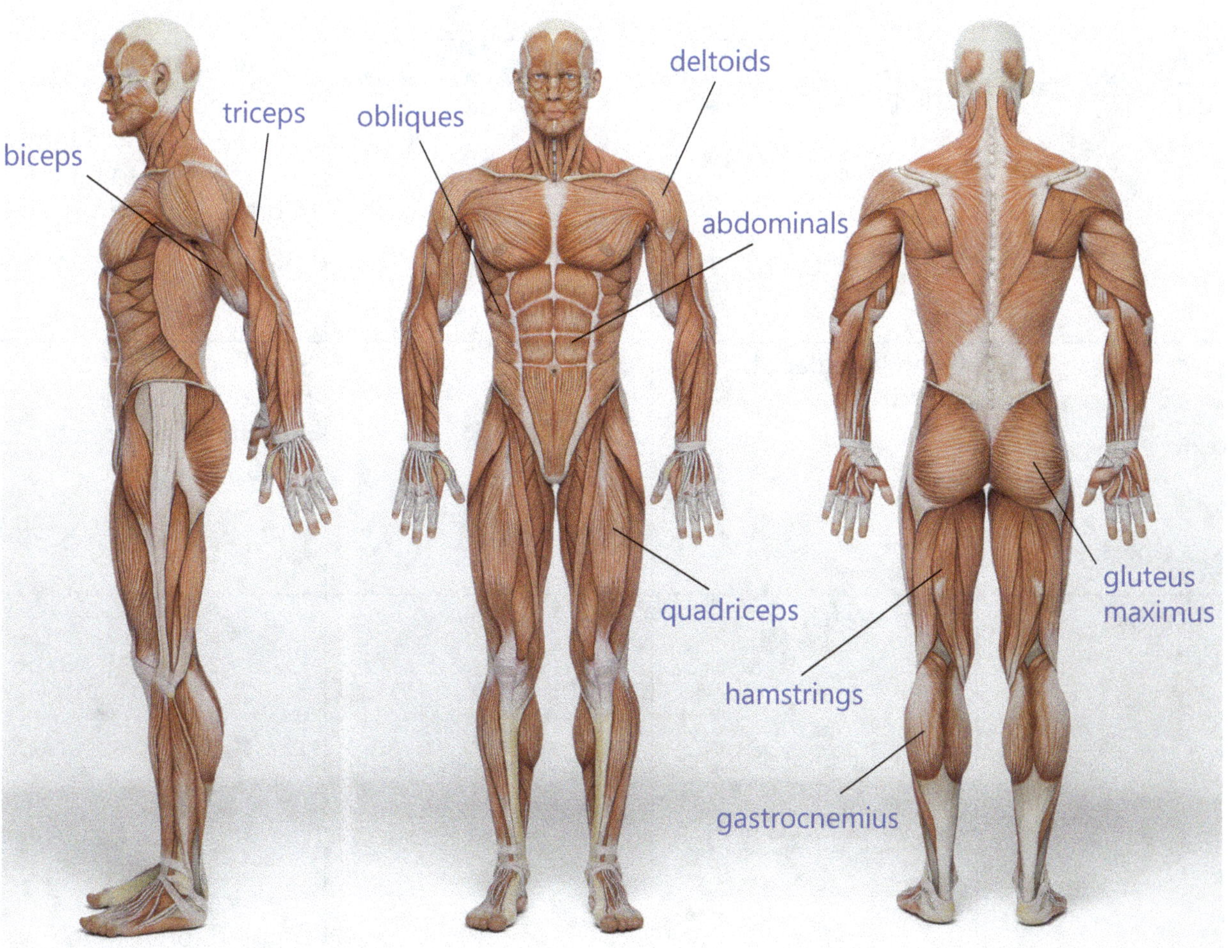

Muscle labels: biceps, triceps, obliques, deltoids, abdominals, quadriceps, hamstrings, gastrocnemius, gluteus maximus

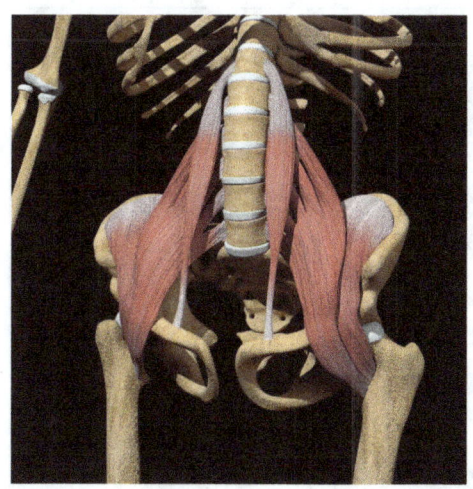

Hip flexors are a number of different muscles used to pull up the thigh. Some quadricep muscles are also counted as hip flexors.

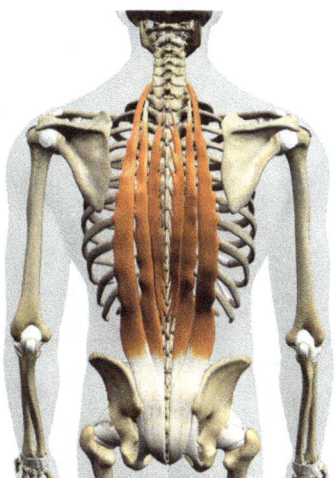

Ererector spinae are muscles along the spine which move and rotate the back.

3 C1 Planning a warm-up

53

Different types of stretch

There are two main types of stretch:

- **static stretch** – this is when the stretch is held in one position
- **dynamic stretch** – this is when the stretch is done whilst moving

Both types of stretch can target:

- one muscle group – this is called a **simple stretch**
- two or more muscle groups – this is called a **compound stretch**.

Muscle group	Static stretch name		Dynamic stretch
deltoids	Deltoid standing stretch		A bear hug – spread arms far apart and then bring them in to hug yourself
biceps	Behind the back bicep stretch		Stand up straight and then gently lower into the static stretch position.
triceps	Tricep stretch		The tricep dip can be adapted for a stretch if the lower position is held
erector spinae	Cat-cow stretch		
abdominals	Back bend		Lying face down on the floor, bring move into the back bend position.

obliques	Sideways full-body stretch		Perform the sideways full-body stretch on one side, and then move through a standing position to the same stretch on the other side
hip flexors	Kneeling hip flexor stretch		From a standing position lower the body into the static kneeling position, then stand up and repeat on other leg.
gluteus maximus	Lying gluteal stretch		Pigeon pose
quadriceps	One-leg standng quadricep stretch		High knees
hamstrings	Standing hamstring stretch		Seated toe touch
gastrocnemius	Calf stretch		Calf raises

Compound stretches

Here are some example of compound stretches.

Compound stretch	Muscle groups		Static or dynamic?
Air squat	quadriceps, hamstrings, gluteus maximus, gastrocnemius		Dynamic
Lunge	gluteus maximus, hamstrings, quadriceps, gastrocnemius, abdominals		Dynamic
Forward leg swing (front to back)	hamstrings, gastrocnemius, quads,		Dynamic
Glute bridges	glutes, hip flexors, abs, obliques		Dynamic
Behind the back shoulder stretch (cow face)	deltoids, triceps		Static
Spinal twist stretch	glutes, abs, obliques, deltoids		Static
Arm swings	biceps and triceps		Dynamic

Response of cardio-respiratory system to preparation stretch

The response depends on whether it is a static or dynamic stretch.

Static stretch

Slight drop in breathing rate as exercise intensity drops

Slight drop in heart rate as exercise intensity drops

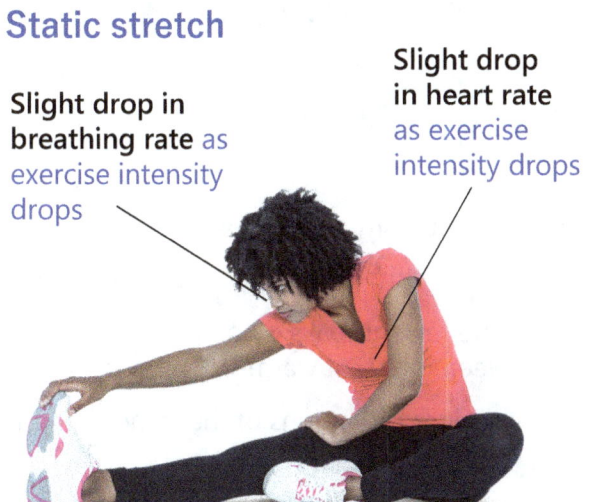

Dynamic stretch

Heart rate remains at a higher level due to the movement in the stretch

Breathing rate remains at a higher level due to the movement in the stretch

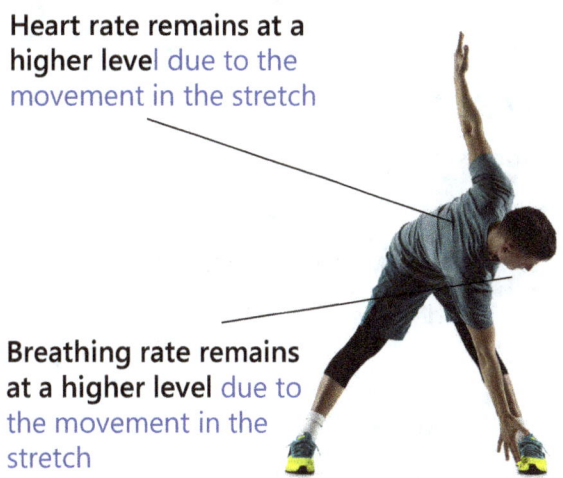

Response of musculoskeletal system to preparation stretch

Stretching muscles makes them longer before exercise begins.

This helps prevent muscles tearing during the physical activity or sport.

Activity

1. Describe the difference between a mobiliser and a preparation stretch.

2. What happens to the cardio-respiratory system during a) a mobiliser b) a preparation stretch?

3. What happens to the musculoskeletal system during a) a mobiliser b) a preparation stretch?

4. a) Describe the difference between a static stretch and a dynamic stretch.

b) Describe the difference between a simple stretch and a compound stretch.

5. Name the muscles labelled A, B and C.

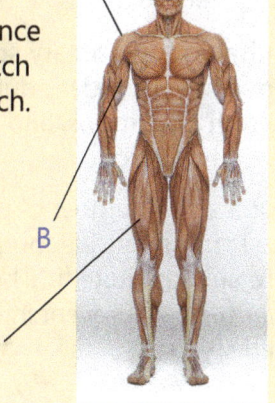

C2 Adapting a warm-up for different types of participants and physical activities

Warm-ups should be adapted for:
- different types of participant
- different types of physical activity.

> **Intro**
> How have your own warm-ups have changed since you were younger?

Adapting warm-ups for different categories of participant

Examples of types of participant include:
- people of different ages:
    * Primary school age (5-11)
    * Adolescents (12-17)
    * Adults (18-49)
    * Older adults (50+)
- people with disabilities
- people with health conditions
- people with different activity levels.

There are a few ways we can adapt warm-ups.

Vary intensity

For some people, a standard warm-up is too intense. Instead of preparing them for exercise, it risks injuring them instead.

For **lower intensity warm-ups**:
- Perform warm-up exercises at a slower pace.
- Include breaks between different warm-up exercises.
- Have fewer repetitions of the same exercise.

Suitable for: primary school age and younger adolescents, older adults (50+), people with health conditions, and people who are not used to exercise.

For a small number of people a standard warm-up is not intense enough. This is because they are already quite fit. They need a more intense warm-up to prevent injury during the physical activity itself.

For **higher intensity warm-ups**:
- Perform warm-up exercises at a faster pace
- Include fewer breaks, or no breaks, between different warm-up exercises
- Have more repetitions of the same exercise

Suitable for: adults who are very fit.

> Note that just because someone is in one category it doesn't mean a standard warm-up for their age is suitable for them. For example:
> - A 30-year-old-man might be quite unfit and lead an unhealthy lifestyle. He would need a lower intensity warm-up.
> - However a very fit 60-year-old-woman would need a higher intensity warm-up.

Low and high impact

Impact is how much pressure an exercise puts on joints.

High-impact exercises put more pressure on joints. Examples of high-impact movements include:

- jumping
- sudden changes in speed
- changes in direction
- any exercise where all the body weight is only supported by one leg (e.g. hopping)

Low impact exercises put less pressure on the joints. Examples of low-impact exercises include:

- squats
- side steps
- bum kicks
- arm circles
- knee lifts
- punches.

For any high-impact warm-up there is a low impact alternative. For example, knee bends and marching instead of jogging for a pulse-raiser

People who are heavier, have weaker muscles, or problems with their joints need low impact warm-ups.

> Note that it is possible to combine higher intensity with low impact. For example, low-impact exercises could be performed quickly or with little rest in between.
>
> Higher intensity but lower impact is suitable for
>
> - older people who are fit
> - fit adults who have problems with some joints
> - fit adults who are recovering from injury.

Vary timing

If a warm-up is less intense then it needs to last longer. This is to make sure that the participant is fully warmed up.

Longer warm-ups are recommended for:

- older adults (50+)
- less-fit adults
- beginners who are not used to exercise.

Types of stretch

There are lots of different muscles in the body. Targeting the correct muscles with the right stretches can be quite hard.

- It is recommended that beginners and less-experienced participants use simple stretches, which only target one muscle group at a time.
- More experienced or advanced participants can use compound stretches, which target several muscle groups at once.

This is because:

- beginners need to learn how to feel which muscles they are targeting in each stretch
- compound stretches are more complicated and could cause injury if done wrong.

Adapting warm-ups to specific physical activities

Warm-ups are meant to prepare the body for a specific activity. Each sport or activity makes use of different movements, muscles and joints. Even different versions of the same activity (e.g. long-distance running versus sprinting) can have a different focus.

We can focus warm-ups on the specific activity by:

- Introducing equipment from the activity or sport into the warm-up – this helps recreate movements and use the correct muscles.
- Using movements from the activity in the warm-up – the joints and muscles used in these movements are the most important to prepare for exercise.
- Stretching the main muscles that will be used in the warm-up – injury is more likely if muscles that are used in the activity have not been warmed up.

Activity – Netball

Equipment that could be used: netball, hoop and netball court

Essential movements: pivoting, catching, throwing, jumping, changes of direction

Pulse-raiser ideas: running and throwing activities, side-steps across the court

Mobiliser: should focus on the joints that are important for running and throwing

Stretches: should focus on important muscles such as deltoids, glutes, quads, gastrocnemius, hip flexors

Activity – Swimming (breaststroke)

Equipment that could be used: swimming pool, floats

Essential movements: arm and leg movements for breaststroke

Pulse-raiser ideas: standing arm rotations, leg-only slow swimming using floats

Mobiliser: should particularly focus on the hip, knee, ankle, shoulder and elbow

Stretches: should focus on important muscles in the lower body, such as hip flexors, glutes, hamstrings, quadriceps, gastrocnemius, as well as the triceps and deltoids

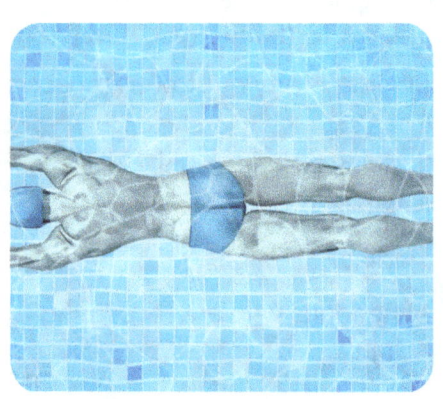

Activity

1. a) What are the advantages and disadvantages of i) static stretches ii) dynamic stretches?

b) What are the advantages and disadvantages of i) simple stretches ii) compound stretches?

2. Why is it important to vary warm-up intensity for different types of participant?

3. a) Why would you choose a low-impact warm-up for a participant?

b) i) Give **two** examples of low-impact pulse-raisers. ii) Give **two** examples of high-impact pulse-raisers.

c) i) Give an example of a high-intensity low-impact pulse-raiser. ii) Who might benefit from this warm-up?

4. a) Identify three muscles that are very important for a football defender. b) Name three different stretches that would target these muscles. In each case, state if the stretch is i) static or dynamic, ii) simple or compound.

5. a) Name three sports where the deltoid muscles are particularly important. b) Describe i) a static stretch ii) a dynamic stretch for the deltoids.

6. What is the name of the muscles in the calf?

7. Explain why warm-ups should be designed with a specific sport or activity in mind.

Lennon is a 21 year old student at university. He plays as a fullback for the university hockey team and also runs a few times a week. His shoulder often feels stiff in cold weather due to an old injury. He has put on more weight recently and his left hip feels sore after a game.

8. a) Name two joints that mobiliser exercises should target for hockey.

b) State three important muscles used in hockey.

c) State three different exercises that could be used to stretch these muscles.

d) i) Explain why it is important to adapt warm-ups for different types of participant.

ii) Describe how you could adapt a warm-up for hockey.

e) Now you need to design a warm-up plan for Lennon. Your plan should include:
- pulse-raiser activities
- mobiliser activities
- preparation stretches
- a description of how much time should be spent on each activity, and each part of the warm-up.

f) Explain why you chose each warm-up activity.

g) i) What effect does each activity have on (**a**) the cardio-respiratory system, (**b**) the musculo-skeletal system? b) Why is this important for Lennon?

h) What modifications did you make, so that the plan was specifically for hockey?

i) What modifications did you make, so that the plan was specifically for Lennon?

C3 Delivering a warm-up to prepare participants for physical activities

Organising and demonstrating warm-up activities

To be effective, a well-planned warm-up also has to be delivered effectively.

To deliver it effectively you need to consider the following.

> **Intro**
>
> Think about the best lessons you have had – what was good about them?

Space

- How much space will you need for all parts of the warm-up?
- Could you use an outdoor area even if the activity is inside?
- Is there space for any equipment for everyone?
- What happens if it rains?

Equipment

Some equipment might be useful:

- cones
- mats, benches or steps
- stopwatch and whistle
- other sport-specific equipment, such as rackets or balls.
- Do you have enough of everything for everyone?

Organising participants

- Will some activities be performed in groups or pairs?
- Can participants help each other with stretches?

Timing

You need to make sure warm-ups are long enough to be effective, but not so long that people get bored or the warm-up becomes less effective.

- Is there enough time to demonstrate, for participants to understand what they need to do, and to do it?
- Is there enough time to increase the intensity in each part of the warm-up?
- Have you factored in any extra time for particular types of participant, who may need longer?
- Have you factored in the time to set up and use any equipment?

Demonstrating and positioning

Demonstrations should be:

- easy for everyone to see and hear
- broken down into key parts
- clearly explained in simple language.

You should demonstrate the each exercise immediately before it is performed.

- Do not demonstrate all the pulse-raisers, mobilisers and stretches all at once, and expect people to remember them!

Can everyone see and hear the instructor?

You should be clearly positioned so everyone can see and hear. If the group is large, or it is noisy, you may have to repeat each demonstration with smaller groups.

Demonstrations should be repeated a few times, to make sure that everyone understands what you are asking them to do.

Teaching points and instructions

Demonstrating techniques is a form of teaching. So you need to consider the best ways to get your points across.

- Your instructions should be clear and easy to understand.
- Break each exercise technique down into its simplest parts.
- Think about how to explain and demonstrate each different part, so that participants do them correctly and safely.
- Use short sentences or key points for each part.
- Do not overload people with information, or explain in lots of detail.
- Use simple language.
- Be clear about what **not** to do too – for example, for a low-impact pulse-raiser you should be clear that at no point should both feet be off the ground at the same time.

Supporting participants taking part in warm-ups

After you have demonstrated each part of the warm-up, participants will try and perform it themselves.

You need to provide help and support as they do so.

Your aim is to makes sure each participant is fully warmed up for their chosen spot or physical activity. You will need to:

- **Observe participants.** You must watch everyone carefully to make sure they are performing each exercise correctly:

* is the technique correct?
* are they at the right intensity?
* are they increasing intensity too quickly/slowly?

- If someone is not doing something correctly you may need to demonstrate it again. You may also need to provide further **instructions** and **teaching points**. Just like in the initial instruction and demonstration, instructions and teaching points should be simple, clear, and broken down into small steps.

- You should **provide feedback** to all participants. Do not get so engrossed in correcting one person's technique that you don't pay attention to other people in the group.

Providing feedback

Your feedback should be constructive. This means you should:

- state what participants are doing well...
- ...but also explain what they could do to improve

You should always aim to encourage performers rather than criticise.

* **what can they improve?**

rather than:

* **what are they doing wrong?**

Your feedback should always keep in mind the ultimate aim: to fully and safely warm-up for the given sport or physical activity.

You should also ask the participants for their feedback during the warm-up:

- Even with the best planning, sometimes the warm-up might be too intense or making people sore.

- You should keep checking in with everyone that they are okay – particularly if they are older or have a health condition.
- If anyone is visibly struggling, or says that they are, they should stop immediately.

Providing feedback is a form of communication. Communication is not jut what we say, it is:

- How we say something (i.e. tone of voice).
- Our facial expression.
- Our general body language.

Assessment

In part 2 of the third assessment task you will need to show that you can deliver your warm-up plan to real participants.

For the best marks:

- Your demonstrations need to be 'effective'.
    * Effective demonstrations would consider and address all of the questions listed on the last three pages.
- The demonstrations should use a 'wide range of appropriate teaching points'.
    * 'Wide range' means that lots of different teaching points should be used throughout the demonstration.
    * 'Appropriate' means that the teaching points suit the participants and situation.
    * For example, some participants may not know the names of different muscles. Describing a stretch using muscle names would not be appropriate for them. A visual aid might help them instead.
- You should provide 'consistent' and 'appropriate support' to all participants:
    * 'Support' means that you are observing all participants as they warm up, correcting them, providing feedback and encouragement, and demonstrating exercises again if needed.
    * 'Consistent' means that you are always providing support, as needed by each participant
    * 'Consistent' also means you should provide the same level of support for the three components of a warm-up, and the different exercises in each component
    * 'Appropriate support' means that each participant receives the right level of help to complete the warm-up fully and appropriately. For example, an experienced and fit 20 year old is likely to need a different level of support than an unfit 30-year-old with a health condition.

The best demonstrations lead to each participant completing a full warm-up that is appropriate for them and their sport or activity.

Component 2 Taking part and improving other participants' sporting performance

In this component you will learn about:

- Components of physical and skill-related fitness, and how they are important in different sports and activities
- Different skills and strategies for different sports
- The roles and responsibilities of officials in sport
- Sporting rules and regulations
- Planning and delivering drills to develop sporting skills

There are three learning outcomes in this component.

A Understand how different components of fitness are used in different physical activities

- A1 Components of physical fitness
- A2 Components of skill-related fitness

B Be able to participate in sport and understand the roles and responsibilities of officials

- B1 Techniques, strategies and fitness required for different sports
- B2 Officials in sport
- B3 Rules and regulations in sports

C Demonstrate ways to improve participants sporting techniques

- C1 Planning drills and conditioned practices to develop participants' sporting skills
- C2 Drills to improve sporting performance

Assessment

This unit is internally assessed. This means that your teacher will mark it. There are 4 tasks in the assessment. These tasks are based around a vocational context that will be provided by your teacher.

A1 Components of physical fitness

Aerobic endurance

The human body needs energy to move. One way we get energy is by using oxygen to break down food.

Our bodies use the **cardiorespiratory** system to transfer oxygen from the air to our cells.

The cardiorespiratory system is made up of the heart and lungs, blood and blood vessels.

Intro

With a partner, take it in turns for one person to jog gently on the spot whilst the other person times them for 1 minute. How long does it take for your breathing to get quicker?

cardio relating to the heart

respiratory relating to breathing

aerobic using oxygen

When we breathe in, we send oxygen to all the cells in our body

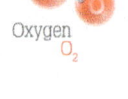

These include the cells that make up muscles

The cardiorespiratory system also removes waste products from our cells

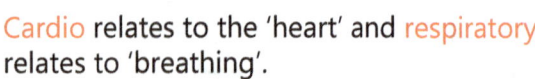

The cells use this oxygen to release energy, which can move our muscles

Cardio relates to the 'heart' and respiratory relates to 'breathing'.

When our bodies get energy using oxygen we call it aerobic. Aerobic means 'using oxygen'.

The cardiorespiratory system provides enough oxygen so that:

- muscles can move at a low or medium level of intensity
- muscles can keep working at this intensity for quite a long time.

Aerobic endurance is how long we can keep performing at a low or medium level of intensity. Aerobic endurance is important for any activity that takes place for more than around 30–90 seconds.

You can tell when an activity is testing your aerobic endurance, because you will begin to feel out of breath.

Aerobic endurance depends on how good the cardiorespiratory system is at getting oxygen to the muscles.

Professional athletes have an excellent cardiorespiratory system. They can perform at a higher intensity, for longer.

This professional marathon runner has a very high aerobic endurance. He can run very fast for more than two hours without stopping.

Muscular endurance

Muscular endurance means how long your muscles can keep working for at low or medium intensity. Muscular endurance is not the same as muscular strength – for that see the next page.

To understand muscular endurance, consider an activity such as a plank. Many people find it hard to do hold a plank for long. At a certain point the stomach and arm muscles can no longer hold the body's weight.

Notice that you don't stop a plank because of aerobic endurance – you are not out of breath. It is because the muscle cannot physically take it any more.

A plank requires good muscular endurance rather than aerobic endurance

Muscular endurance allows you to use a muscle at low or medium intensity for quite a long period of time. It is important in many sports and physical activities. For instance, muscular endurance is important for:

- kicking a ball in a football or rugby match
- serving throughout a long tennis match
- supporting the body's weight when rock climbing.

There are many different muscles in the human body. Muscular endurance is different for different groups of muscles. For instance:

- a professional rower has excellent muscular endurance in their arms, shoulders and back
- a professional cyclist has excellent muscular endurance in their legs and buttocks.

Muscular endurance can be measured by how many exercise repetitions someone can do, rather than the heaviest weight they can lift or move.

Activity

1. List i) one team sport, ii) one individual sport, and iii) one activity, where aerobic endurance is important.

2. List i) one team sport, ii) one individual sport, and iii) one activity, where muscular endurance is important.

3. a) Explain why aerobic endurance is important for a football player.

b) Explain the impact of aerobic endurance on the performance of a football player.

4. a) Explain why a tennis player needs to have muscular endurance.

b) Explain the impact of muscular endurance on a tennis player's performance.

Muscular strength

The largest force that a muscle or group of muscles can produce is called **muscular strength**.

An example of muscular strength would be the heaviest weight that someone can lift in a single bench press.

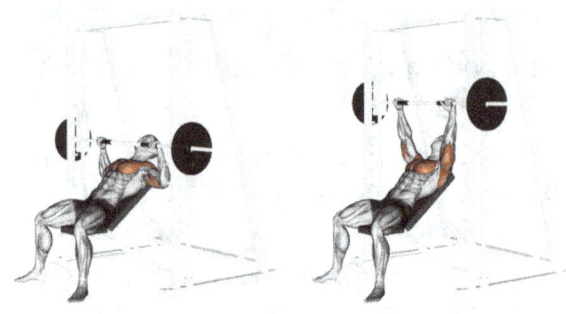

A shot putter with low muscular strength would not be able to throw the shot very far.

This gymnast needs very high levels of upper body muscular strength to lift and support their body weight.

Intro

With a partner discuss which muscle in the human body you think is the strongest.

Muscular strength depends on the size of muscles but also on the way the brain controls the muscle.

Speed

Speed means how quickly something can move.

It is measured by how far something travels in a certain amount of time. For instance, a world-class male sprinter can run 100m in 10 seconds. This means they cover 10m every second. Their speed is 10 metres per second.

In some sports or activities, it is important that the whole body moves quickly.

In races, such as slalom downhill skiing and sprinting, speed is vital.

Speed is also important in team sports such as American football.

In other sports or activities only a part of the body needs to move quickly.

In tennis the serving arm must move very quickly.

A kicker in rugby must move their kicking leg very fast.

In the javelin, the throwing arm must move quickly.

Activity

1. List i) three team sports, ii) three individual sports, where speed is important.

2. List i) three team sports, ii) three individual sports, where muscular strength is important.

3. What is the impact of muscular strength on the performance of a rock climber?

4. Describe the activities within a game of badminton which benefit from movement at high speed.

Flexibility

Each joint in the body has a range of movements.

Flexibility is being able to move a joint through its full range of movements, without feeling any pain.

Even the most flexible joint can only move within limits. For instance, the knee only bends one way – even a very flexible person can only bend their knee so far.

Flexibility can be different for each joint. For instance, someone might have a very flexible elbows and shoulders but less flexible hips.

Flexibility is particularly important for some sports and activities, such as gymnastics and yoga.

Intro

With a partner discuss how flexible you think you are.

Being flexible is also important in everyday life. A person who is not very flexible will be more restricted in their movements.

Flexibility is affected by the condition of ligaments, tendons and muscles associated with each joint. It is also affected by other factors – for instance, flexibility decreases with age.

Flexibility can be improved by stretching.

See Component 1 C1 for more on different types of stretching.

Body composition

Your body is made up of a number of different things. Together all of these things make up your overall **body mass**.

Body mass can be broken down into two main categories:

- mass due to body fat
- mass due to everything else – this includes bones, water and muscle.

Body composition refers to how much of the overall mass is due to body fat and how much is due to everything else.

- Training and exercise tends to reduce the mass due to body fat and increase the mass due to muscle.
- A lack of exercise tends to reduce the mass due to muscle and increase the mass due to body fat.

Different sports and activities suit different body compositions.

Second row rugby players typically have a higher level of body fat and a lot of muscle. Body fat helps to cushion the body from impacts during the game.

Long-distance runners typically have an extremely low level of body fat.

Activity

1. List i) one team sport, ii) one individual sport, and iii) one activity, where flexibility is important.

2. For each of your answers to question 1, describe how flexibility helps performance.

3. Describe i) one Olympic sport that benefits from a higher level of body fat, ii) one Olympic sport that benefits from a lower level of body fat. Justify your answers.

A2 Components of skill-related fitness

Power

In sport and fitness, **power** combines strength and speed.

Power is calculated as force multiplied by speed.

A muscular force applied at high speed produces explosive movement. This can be movement of the body or of another object.

Intro

Discuss why a powerful kick is important in football.

Power is really important in a long jump. The more power in the launching leg upon takeoff, the further the jump.

The start is really important in sprinting. The fastest starters provide the most power out of the starting blocks.

To shoot from distance in football a player needs to kick the ball hard. They need to move their kicking leg very quickly and apply a large force to the ball. Applying this large force quickly generates a high level of power.

Agility

Agility is a measure of a person's ability to change direction and speed quickly.

Agility is more important than outright speed in many sports.

Tennis requires a high level of agility. Players need to constantly change direction and produce short bursts of speed.

Agility is also important in other sports such as basketball.

A basketball court is relatively small, so players must have good agility levels to change direction and dribble past opposing players.

Activity

1. Describe the difference between strength and power.
2. List i) one team sport, ii) one individual sport, iii) one activity, where power is important.
3. Explain how power affects performance in hockey.
4. a) What is the definition of agility? b) Explain why agility is less important in the 1500m than it is in squash.

Reaction time

Reaction time is how quickly someone can respond to an external event. An external event is called a stimulus. In sport a stimulus is normally:

- something you see
- something you hear
- something you feel.

Intro

Write down (in fractions of a second) what you think your own reaction time is.

When you react to a stimulus, certain things happen in the body. Let us think about what happens to a runner at the start of a running race:

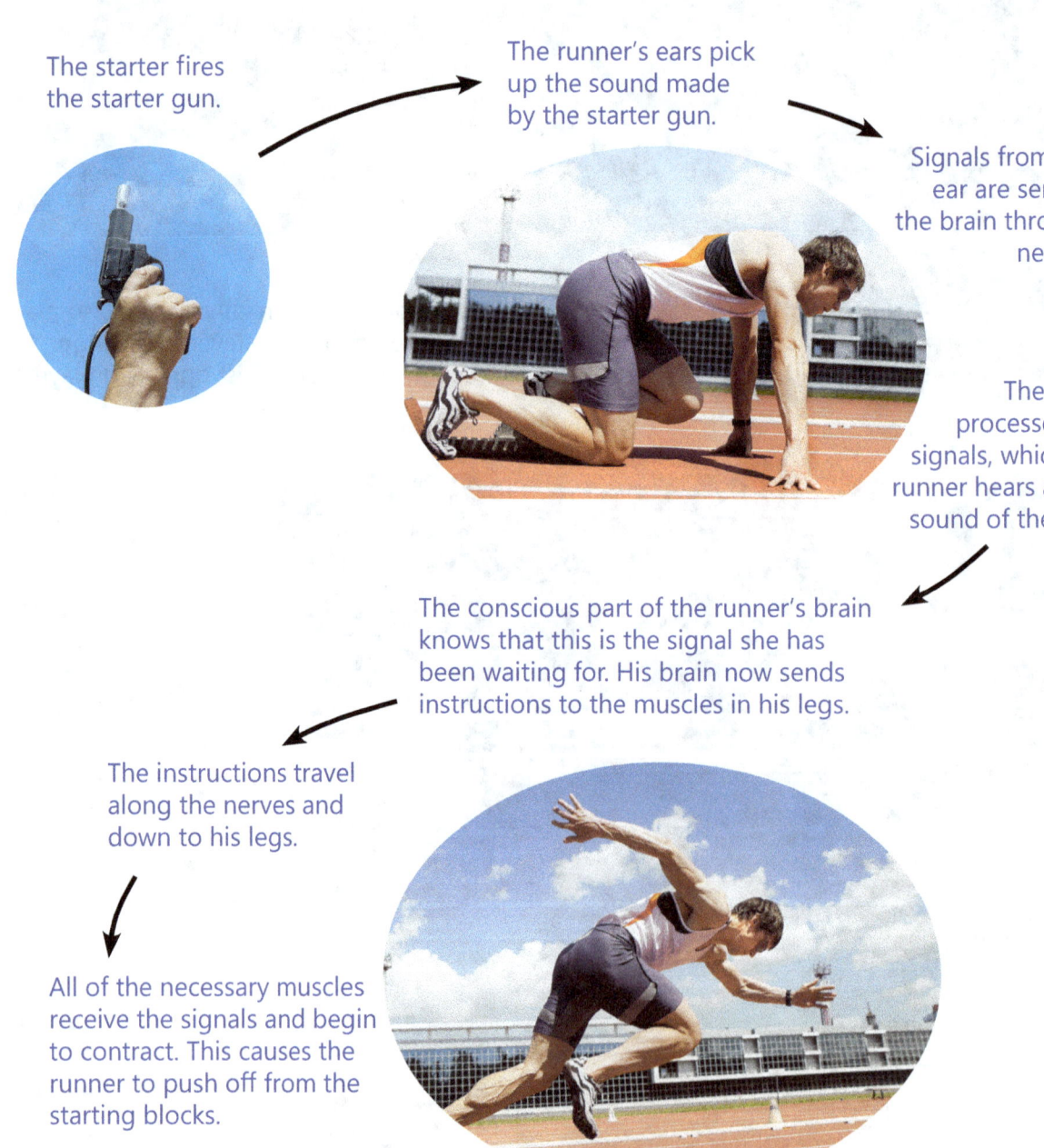

The starter fires the starter gun.

The runner's ears pick up the sound made by the starter gun.

Signals from the ear are sent to the brain through nerves.

The brain processes the signals, which the runner hears as the sound of the gun.

The conscious part of the runner's brain knows that this is the signal she has been waiting for. His brain now sends instructions to the muscles in his legs.

The instructions travel along the nerves and down to his legs.

All of the necessary muscles receive the signals and begin to contract. This causes the runner to push off from the starting blocks.

All of these processes take a certain amount of time. Together, they make up the reaction time between hearing the gun and pushing off the blocks.

Reaction time is critical in a 100m sprint because the race is so short. A runner with a slow reaction time may never be able to make up the time that they lost at the start.

In cricket a batter has to have very quick reaction times to respond to changes in direction of the ball after it bounces.

Reaction times can vary depending on the stimulus and the action. They also vary with age and experience of an event.

- an average reaction time for something you see is a around a quarter of a second (0.25 seconds)
- an average reaction time for something you hear is quicker, at around 0.17 seconds
- sports people and gamers (including e-sports) will normally have faster than average reaction times.

- In athletics sprint events, if an athlete starts the race less than one-tenth of a second (0.1 seconds) after the gun, they are given a false start. This is because it is physically impossible for a human to react that quickly.

Coordination

Coordination means being able to move and position two or more parts of the body at the same time. Coordinated movements are smooth and efficient, not jerky.

Effective sports and fitness techniques need a high level of coordination.

Good coordination is needed to respond to other moving objects or people. This requires hand-eye or foot-eye coordination For example:

- striking a ball in softball
- performing a tackle in football.

Good coordination is also needed to carry out a series of complicated moves, like those in the long jump.

Balance

Balance is the ability to stay upright. Balance depends on two things: the centre of mass and the base of support.

The **centre of mass** of an object is the point around which all mass is equally balanced.

- For a symmetrical object like a ball, the centre of mass is in the exact centre of the object
- For irregular shapes, like the human body, the centre of mass is not in the centre of the body.

The position of the centre of mass depends on the shape of the body. Bending, stretching, and the position of the arms and legs all affect its position. The centre of mass can even be outside the body.

When standing, the **base of support** (BOS) is the area enclosed by the feet. The size of the base of support depends on how wide apart the feet are.

Static balance is being able to stay upright – not fall over – when not moving. Static balance is achieved when the centre of mass is above the base of support.

Static balance is important in sports and activities such as yoga, Tai Chi and gymnastics.

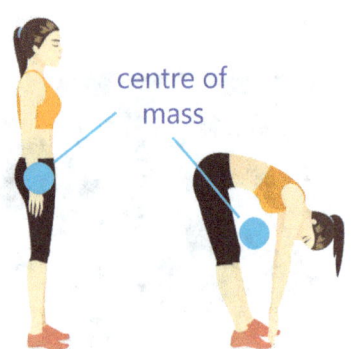

In the photo on the left, the woman has a wide base of support and her centre of mass is low. This means she is balanced and very stable.

In the photo on the right, the woman has moved position. Now she has a narrow base of support, and her centre of mass is higher. She is still balanced, as the centre of mass is still within her base of support. But if she were to move slightly, her centre of mass would be outside her base of support and she would begin to fall. This is a less stable pose than in the first photo.

This swimmer is in a position where his centre of mass lies outside his base of support. He is no longer in static balance, and this causes him to begin moving. In this case he purposely lost static balance in order to move.

Dynamic balance is being able to stay upright while moving. This can be done by repositioning the body, particularly the arms and legs, to shift the centre of mass and the base of support.

Dynamic balance is important in any sport or activity which involves movement. Examples include skateboarding, ice hockey and badminton.

Balance is a surprisingly complicated system that involves our eyes, our ears, movement sensors in our body, and our muscles.

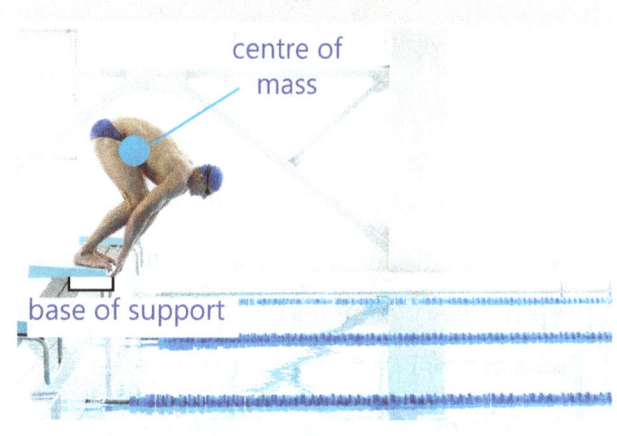

Activity

1. List one skill or technique in football where reaction time is critical.

2. a) Define the term coordination. b) What might happen to a performer in tennis with poor coordination?

3. a) Explain what the terms Centre of Mass and Base of Support mean. b) List i) one team sport, ii) one individual sport, iii) one activity, where balance is important. c) For each answer, describe how balance affects performance.

B1 Techniques, strategies and fitness for sports

Skills

All sports require competitors to perform certain actions and techniques. These are called **skills**.

Skills can be categorised in each of the following ways:

- **simple** or **complex**
- **open** or closed
- **self-paced** or **externally paced**
- **discrete**, **serial** or **continuous**

Most sports need a number of different skills. Each skill may be categorised differently.

> **Intro**
>
> In 1 minute, list all the skills you can think of that are needed in basketball.

Complexity

Skills range from simple to complex. To perform at a high level, a competitor must master the complex skills in their chosen sport.

Simple skills are the building blocks of each sport. Some simple skills are the same in a range of different sorts. Participants need to learn practice and master these simple skills before moving on to more complex skills. For example:

- catching a ball in cricket, softball, rounders and baseball
- kicking a stationary ball in football
- performing a head-first dive from a 1m board in diving.

Complex skills tend to be specific to each sport. The most complex are made up of a number of different parts and require the performer to process information and make decisions. For example:

- spin bowling in cricket
- scoring a goal from a free kick over a wall of defenders
- performing a forward 4½ somersault in diving.

Lots of skills fall somewhere in between simple and complex.

SIMPLE ⟷ COMPLEX

Open and closed skills

The performance of skills may be influenced by the environment. The environment can include other competitors, the weather and the terrain.

Open skills depend on changes in the environment. Performers have to adapt the skill according to what is happening at that moment. For example:

- a return in badminton completely depends on the opponent's serve
- dribbling in football depends on the position, speed, skill and number of opponents.

Closed skills are performed in a predictable environment. The performance of the skill does not have to be adapted. This means that performing the skill in competition will be just like it was in training.

- a floor routine in gymnastics
- the long jump (does not depend on other competitors but does depend on wind direction and speed).

Most skills have some closed and open aspects. It is not simply a choice of one or the other. The diagram shows where some skills lie on the line between open and closed skills. For example, taking a corner in football is partly closed, because the ball is always played from the same point, but partly open, as the player will deliver the ball differently depending on the opponents strengths and positions.

When sports are performed under pressure in front of spectators, even a mostly closed skill can be impacted by this environment.

CLOSED  **OPEN**

Pacing

A **self-paced skill** is one where a performer has control over when they perform it. For example,

- a high-jumper controls when they begin their routine, how quickly they run and the point at which they begin the jump
- a penalty taker in rugby decides when to begin their run and when to kick the ball.

An **externally-paced skill** is one where external factors determine when the skill is performed. Often these external factors are other competitors. For example,

- a defensive intercept in netball can only be executed when an opponent throws the ball
- a routine in figure skating, where the skater's routine is in time to the music.

Self-paced skills tend to be on the closed end of the spectrum. However this is not always the case – for instance the start of the 200m sprint is externally paced (depends on the starter's gun) but the launch off the starting blocks is largely a closed skill.

SELF-PACED ⟷ **EXTERNALLY PACED**

Discrete, serial and continuous

Discrete skills have a clear beginning and end. For example, swinging a golf club to hit the ball.

Serial skills also have a beginning and end but are made up of a number of discrete skills. For example, the actions involved in the triple jump.

Continuous skills are repeated and have no clear beginning or end. For example, there is no clear end to the actions involved in running – the execution of the skill just repeats.

A skilled competitor is someone who can perform skills consistently, at a high standard, in a competitive situation.

DISCRETE ⟷ SERIAL ⟷ CONTINUOUS

Activity

1. Draw two-headed arrows for the skill categories: a) Complexity, b) Open/closed, c) Pacing, d) Discrete/serial/continuous.

Place the skills below on each of the two-headed arrows:

- a penalty kick in rugby
- a penalty save in football
- a javelin throw
- the start of a 50m breaststroke race
- a 10km cross-country race.

2. What skills are important in your chosen sport? List five skills.

Strategies

Whilst skills are critical for each sport, strategies and tactics can also give performers a competitive advantage.

Strategies are the aims for a particular match, event, race, or season. **Tactics** are the way in which the strategy can be carried out.

Intro

In 1 minute think of different tactics a League One football team could use when playing a Premier League club in the FA Cup.

For example, consider a tennis player planning their next singles match on clay. After analysing their opponent's past performance, they decide that:

- the opponent has a very good serve
- their backhand is weaker than their forehand
- they do not like long rallies or long matches.

The strategy for this match is to aim to return as many first serves as possible, play to the backhand as often as possible, and keep the rallies going for as long as possible.

In order to carry out this strategy, the tactics for this match might be:

- Return first serves at all costs, keeping the point alive. Do not try to hit winners from first serves. The main thing is to make sure the opponent has to play another shot.
- Use sliced block returns with the continental grip on the fastest first serves.
- On second serves, aggressively target the opponent's backhand and go for some winners.
- Use slice on groundstrokes to keep the ball in play. The aim is for long rallies to tire your opponent out over the course of the match.
- Use topspin on winners aimed at the backhand.

PLAYER 1	6-4 6-3 5-7	PLAYER 2
	MATCH TIME: 2:20	
7	ACES	6
0	DOUBLE FAULTS	1
60	1st SERVE IN %	45
80	1st SERVE PTS WON %	74
56	2nd SERVE PTS WON %	44
15	WINNERS	19
12	UNFORCED ERRORS	12
8/9	NET POINTS WON	3/13
2/6	BREAK POINTS WON	3/5

TENNIS STATISTICS

Data like this is used to analyse a tennis player's strengths and weaknesses

Decision making

While the strategy and tactics can be planned in advance, the performer still has to decide exactly when to do what. This is called **decision making**.

In our tennis example the player has to decide exactly which second serves to try to hit winners on. They would also have to decide when a rally has gone on for long enough and when to try and win the point.

If the original tactics are not working, the performer, coach or manager might need to change them during the performance. A change of tactics can be planned for. But a good sportsperson can tweak tactics as they perform, to respond to the conditions and opponent.

In our tennis example:

- The opponent may set up shots so that they are returned to her forehand. This prevents her backhand from being targeted and prevents that tactic from working.

- Our player must then decide how to deal with this.

- She notices that her opponent still wants to end rallies quickly and goes for winning shots early in the rally. These sometimes hit the net if she is behind the baseline but are often winners from just inside the baseline.

- Our player decides to change tactics: she will aim to keep her opponent behind the baseline by continuing to use lots of slice. She will then wait for a mistake but will also sometimes surprise her opponent by going for a winner on the forehand, or by playing some drop shots.

In doubles tennis, players can often be seen discussing and changing tactics during the match.

Activity

1. Explain the difference between a strategy and a tactic.

2. Pep Guardiola is famous for managing football teams who have a certain style of play. Research some of the strategies and tactics he has used in some of his teams.

3. Describe two different strategies and tactics that are common in your chosen sport.

Isolated practice

Isolated practice is when you only focus on one skill, or a selection of related skills. Examples of isolated practice include:

- tackle practice in rugby using tackle bags
- batting and bowling practice using cricket nets
- improving sprinting technique using mini hurdles.

Isolated practice allows a sportsperson to concentrate on one skill at a time and improve it. There are a number of benefits of isolated practice:

- It removes the pressure of competing – it doesn't matter if the skill is performed well, the aim is to get better.
- Skills that are not used that much in a real match or competition can be practised over and over. For instance, volleys in tennis are much rarer in tennis than groundstrokes and serves.
- It allows performers to concentrate on things they are not good at – for instance, a football player can practise with their weaker leg.

The disadvantages of isolated practice are:

- The conditions are not realistic – top footballers may score penalties easily in training, but even the very best can miss penalties in highly-pressured games.
- It is hard to recreate situations which require open skills. For instance, a 1500m runner can train to pace their laps perfectly,

Intro

What skills do you think you will need to demonstrate in your chosen sport?

but it is quite different in a race when an opponent unexpectedly kicks with 600m left to run.

- Linked to the point above, a sportsperson cannot recreate decision-making and using tactics in isolated practice.

Competitive situation

In the assessment task you will also need to demonstrate sport skills and strategies in a competitive situation.

A competitive situation could be a practice match, game or event. It should resemble a real match, game or event by having:

- the right number of players/competitors
- the correct pitch, court or other area of play
- a referee or official.

Practice matches are a good way to demonstrate open skills, strategies and decision-making.

A competitive situation allows you to demonstrate open skills, which depend on other competitors' actions.

Assessment

In the second task of the assessment for Component 2, you will need to demonstrate skills for a sport in isolated practice and in competitive situations. When demonstrating these skills, you will need to display high levels of accuracy, fluency and control:

- **Accuracy** – This means that the execution of the skill does what you intended it to. For instance, hitting a forehand in tennis with topspin is an example of a skill. However, if you can hit a forehand with topspin, but it goes out of the court or hits the net, then the skill has not been performed accurately.

- **Fluency** – This means that skill is performed smoothly, in one continuous movement. Movements should not be jerky or ragged.

- **Control** – This means that the skill does not look forced, and the body's movements are efficient. A skill under control can be repeated in the same way many times. A skill that is out of control is likely to look different each time it is performed.

You will also need to show your understanding and use of strategies and tactics in a competitive situation. For the very best marks you will need to **select and perform appropriate strategies effectively**, in all situations.

- **Select and perform appropriate strategies** means that you choose the right strategy at the right time.

- **Effectively** means that the strategies actually work in practice e.g. to win a point or outwit an opponent.

To prepare for this part of the assessment you should:

- Choose a sport you are good at.

- Write down five skills that are used in that sport. For example, it could be serve, forehand, backhand, lob, and drop shot in badminton.

- Ask yourself which of these skills you are best at. Put the skills in order, from best to worst.

- Think about how easy or hard it will be for you to demonstrate these skills in isolated practice and in a competitive situation. Remember that your skill demonstrations should be accurate, fluent and controlled.

- Choose the skills you think will be the best to demonstrate and focus on these for your assessment.

For the same sport brainstorm as many different strategies as you can in five minutes. It might help to do this in pairs or small groups. Now think about:

- **How often these strategies can be demonstrated in a game or match.** For example, long throw-ins in football can be used to get the ball into the penalty area. But this strategy only works if the ball goes out of play in certain areas of the pitch. This might not happen that often.

- **How appropriate these strategies are for your demonstration.** For example, long throw-ins only make sense if a) you have someone who can throw the ball a long way and b) you have tall players who can win the ball in the penalty area.

- **How easy or hard it will be to demonstrate each strategy in a game or match.** Complicated strategies might be hard for other players in the game to understand, and it might be hard for an observer to see what is happening.

B2 Officials in sport

Roles of officials

Officials in sport are responsible for:

- making sure the rules of the sport are followed
- ruling on decisions during the event –
- keeping score
- handing out punishments if rules are broken
- organising competitors.

Officials must be unbiased and impartial.

Referees and umpires

The main person in charge of a sporting event is called the umpire or referee. Different sports use different terms, for example:

- **Umpire**: cricket, tennis, netball, hockey
- **Referee**: football, rugby, volleyball

The responsibilities of a referee or umpire are different in each sport:

- They make sure that the rules of the sport are being followed.
- They make the final call on decisions during the event – for instance, deciding which team has control of the ball after it has gone out of play.
- They hand out punishments if rules are broken.

Intro

In one minute write down all the sports you can think of that use umpires.

It is difficult for a single referee or umpire to see everything during a game or event. So they often have other officials to help them. However the referee or umpire always has the final say, and can overrule their assistants.

Assistant referee and line umpires

Assistant referees have specific responsibilities but can also inform the referee if they see any infringements.

For example, in rugby union a touch judge checks if the ball or player goes out of touch, and whether a conversion has been scored. But they can also signal to the referee that a player has committed foul play.

Racket sports use line umpires to check whether the ball or shuttlecock has gone out of play. It is a very skilled role and line judges often concentrate on just one line of the court. This means that many line judges are needed for professional matches.

Judges

In some sports competitors are awarded points by **judges**. The judges score the competitors against certain standards. For instance, in diving the competitors' scores are based on:

- the difficulty of the dive
- how well the dive was performed.

Judges are highly skilled but their scores are subjective – different judges will score the same dive slightly differently. For this reason, the final score is the average of several judges' scores.

Some other sports that use judges include:

- rhythmic gymnastics
- figure skating
- synchronised swimming
- diving
- dressage
- skateboarding
- freestyle BMX
- boxing
- freestyle snowboarding.

Scorers

High-scoring sports have an official **scorer** to keep track of the score. This allows the main referee or umpire to concentrate on the action.

Scorers are present in basketball, baseball, handball, volleyball and cricket.

Timekeepers

In some sports a separate official keeps track of the length of the game or match. They are also responsible for stopping the clock during any breaks in play. Some sports that use **timekeepers** in this way are: netball, basketball, boxing and futsal.

Timekeepers are key officials for any kind of race, such as in athletics, cycling or motorsport. Whilst sophisticated timing equipment is used for elite events, a manual timekeeper is still important at amateur events. A timekeeper may also start a race. Alternatively, the **starter** can be a separate role.

Video review officials

Many professional sports now use video technology to check important decisions during an event. A video review official's role is to look at replays whilst the event is taking place, and alert the referee or umpire if there appear to be any incorrect decisions.

Different sports use different systems:

- The TMO system in rugby union. TMO can check if there were any infringements in the build-up to a try, and for fouls during general play.

- The VAR system in football. VAR checks all the major events in a game, such as goals, penalties and red cards.

- The DRS in cricket. As well as video replays, this system also uses audio (to detect if a ball hit the edge of the bat) and ball-tracking technology (to check for LBW)

- In fencing, a video referee aids the main referee with scoring decisions

VIDEO ASSISTANT REFEREES

Activity

1. List the main officials in

   a) rugby league

   b) badminton

   c) netball.

2. For each of your answers in question 1, list the main things that each official does during a game or match.

See page 43 (Component 1) for more on video-assisted decision making.

Officials' responsibilities in sport

Officials in sport have a number of responsibilities.

Appearance

Officials make sure that the competitors are wearing the right clothing. Examples include:

- Swimmers must wearing swimming caps during races.
- Footballers must wear shinpads.
- Triathletes must wear wetsuits below a certain water temperature, and must not wear them above a certain temperature.
- When two teams compete against each other at the same time (e.g. hockey) then they should wear different colours.
- The official also has to wear clothes that follow the rules of the sport. They should be easily seen and must not wear colours that could confuse them for a participant.

Intro

In 1 minute write down all the different things you think a football referee does during a match.

Equipment

Officials check that any equipment used in the competition follows the rules of the sport. For example:

- Boxer's gloves are checked before a bout, to make sure they are in excellent condition and that the laces are tied and covered.
- The studs on rugby and football boots have a maximum length and must not be sharp.
- There are rules about the length, height and width of professional cyclists' bicycles.
- Track athletes' shoes must have a certain number of spikes, in certain positions.

Officials are also required to carry equipment to carry out their roles. Examples include:

- a whistle in basketball
- red and yellow cards in football
- measuring tape in the long jump and triple jump
- starter pistol in track events.

Effective communication

It is very important that officials can:

- consult with other officials, to make sure they all have a clear understanding of events in the match or game
- communicate decisions clearly, so everyone knows what is happening
- explain their decisions, so competitors can understand what rules are being applied.

Different types of communication include:

- speaking – tone of voice as well as choice of words
- listening
- body language – for instance an aggressive stance or not looking someone in the eye
- using flags or gestures that have specific meanings in the sport.

All of these can affect the way a player, or other officials, receive a message.

Effective communication can help a game or event run smoothly.

Control of players

Emotions can run high in sport. This can lead to poor behaviour and rule breaking. Officials have to control this. This might mean:

- a stern warning
- punishment, as per the rules of the sport
- removal from the playing area.

Effective communication can help control players and prevent conflict. However some players will behave poorly no matter what. Officials need to address this..

While the officials have a responsibility to control players, the main responsibility is on the players to control themselves.

Fitness requirements

Some officials need high levels of fitness to keep up with the location of the action. These officials need to pass certain fitness tests in

order to perform their role. Fitness standards increase for elite level officials. Examples include:

- interval fitness tests in football, to make sure referees can do lots of short sprints with recovery
- change of direction tests in futsal, to make sure referees can react to the quick movements of the ball
- the British Basketball League states that referees have to complete 86 laps of a bleep fitness test.

Health and safety

All sports have some degree of risk. Officials need to consider the health and safety of all participants, officials and spectators at all times.

Examples of officials' health and safety actions include:

- Ensuring the sporting environment is safe (e.g. the running track is not icy).
- Stopping play if the environment has become unsafe (e.g. if a flare is thrown onto a football pitch).
- Ensuring all equipment and clothing complies with all rules (e.g. removing jewellery).
- Following concussion protocols in rugby, where head injuries are very dangerous.
- Removing players who have endangered other players.
- Signalling for medical staff if a competitor is injured or unwell.
- Ensuring throwing and landing areas are safe and clear of people in events such as the hammer, discus and javelin.
- Using yellow flags, safety cars and red flags to prevent accidents in motorsport.

Activity

1. List all of the officials in field hockey.

2. Choose one of the officials from question 1. Using full sentences, describe three of the official's responsibilities.

3. Look at each of the responsibilities in this section (Appearance, Equipment, Effective Communication and so on). Give an example of an official demonstrating each responsibility. You can choose an official from any sport, but each example should be from a different sport.

B3 Rules and regulations in sport

All sports have rules and regulations to make sure the sport is fair and safe. They are also designed to make the competition interesting.

The National Governing Bodies are in charge of rules and regulations. At a professional level they cover every aspect of competing in the sport. However, rules can still vary between different competitions run by the same NGB.

> **Intro**
>
> Choose a sport and write down all the rules you can think of in 1 minute.

Number of players

The number of players in a team impacts how the sport is played. It can be broken down into:

- The number of players competing at the same time.
- The number and type of substitutions.

Substitutes can be fixed or rolling:

- Fixed substitutes mean there are a maximum number of substitutes, who are only allowed onto the playing area at certain times.
- Rolling substitutes can return to the playing area.

For example, in English Premier League football:

- 11 players are allowed on the pitch for each team at any time, and one must be the goalkeeper
- Each team must have 7 or more players on the field at all times.
- There can be up to 5 substitutions, from up to 9 players on the bench. Teams can only stop play three times to make substitutions.

Ice hockey allow rolling substitutes. However, football has strict limits on how many substitutes can be used.

Different formats of sports can have different numbers of people. For example:

- 5-aside football played under FA rules has 5 players and 3 rolling substitutes
- Rugby Sevens has 7 players and 3 fixed substitutes.

Different rules can apply in different competitions. Whilst the Premier League and EFL moved to 5 substitutes, the National League (tiers 5 and 6 of the football pyramid) stuck with 3 substitutes. Similarly, amateur football, Sunday league and youth competitions run by the FA will have some slightly different rules to the Premier League.

Wheelchair basketball allows rolling substitutes from a bench of 7 players.

	Max number of players per team on playing area	Substitutions
Rugby Union	15	8 fixed, from a bench of 8 players. Some of these players must be for specialised positions.
Rugby League	13	8 rolling from a bench of 4 players
Basketball	5	Rolling, with different numbers of players on the bench in different competitions
Wheelchair Basketball	5	Rolling, from a bench of 7 players
Volleyball	6	Rolling, from a bench of 6 players. But returning players can only swap with their substitute
Beach volleyball	2	0
Sitting volleyball (international rules)	6	Rolling, from a bench of 6 players. But returning players can only swap with their substitute

Playing time

In most sports the playing time can be organised in two different ways:

1. By score. In these sports each period of play continues until a particular score is reached. The match is over when an overall score is reached. Examples include:

- badminton
- squash
- snooker.

2. By time. These sports are often broken down into equal periods of play. Examples include:

- football – two halves of 45 minutes, plus time added on for any stoppages.
- ice hockey – three periods of 20 minutes.
- American football – four quarters of 15 minutes.

In certain situations, further periods of play are required in order to declare a winner:

- If a football match is tied after 90 minutes in a knockout tournament, there are two further 15-minute periods of play. If the score is still tied after that then the match is decided with a penalty shootout.

- In badminton, if a player reaches 21 points but does not lead by 2 points, the game carries on until someone has a 2-point lead or reaches 30 points.

- In ice hockey, if the match is tied after three periods then an additional overtime period is played. If the match is still tied after that then there is a shootout.

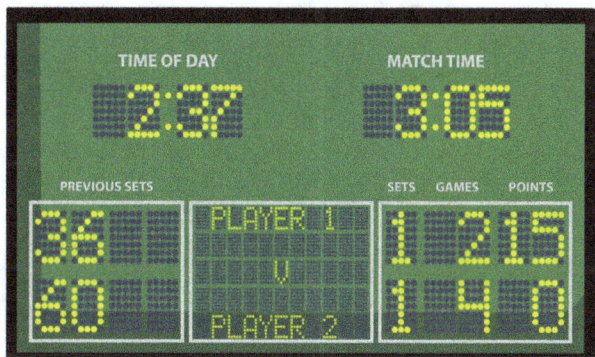

In sports like tennis, the playing time depends on the score.

Activity

This question is about American football.

1. a) Describe the rules about the number of players

b) Explain how substitutions work.

c) What are the rules about playing time?

d) i) What do the officials do to make sure all these rules are followed correctly?

e) Are there different rules in different competitions (for example, NFL and College Football)?

Scoring

There are lots of different ways that sports are scored. We can group some similar sports together.

Racket sports

Examples include: tennis, badminton, squash and padel.

- In these sports, points are awarded when the ball (or shuttlecock) is not returned or goes out of play.
- The first player to win a certain number of points wins the game or set.
- The first player to win a certain number of games or sets wins the match.

Basket, net and line sports

Examples include: basketball, netball, football, ice hockey, rugby, lacrosse and American football.

- In these sports points are awarded for putting a ball within a net, basket or hoop, or crossing over a line.
- The aim is to get a higher score than the opponent.
- Some sports use a simple scoring system, where achieving the objective is worth one point, no matter how it is scored. For example, in football a goal is only ever worth one point.
- Some sports use a more complex scoring system, where different points are awarded in different circumstances. For example:
  * In basketball, baskets are worth 3 points if thrown from outside the 3-point line, and 2 points if thrown inside. A basket scored from the free throw line is worth 1 point.
  * In American football, a touchdown is worth 6 points, a field goal is worth 3 points, and a conversion is worth 1 or 2 points depending on how it is done.

Intro

Choose a racket sport and write down everything you know about the scoring rules.

Table tennis scoring system.

In both codes of rugby, different points are awarded for conversions and penalties.

Batting sports

Examples include: cricket, baseball, rounders and softball.

- In these sports, the objective is to hit a ball with a bat. This allows the team to score points.
- Points may be scored because the batting was so good, for example in cricket when hitting the ball to the boundary scores 4 runs.
- Points may be scored by running somewhere whilst the ball is retrieved. For example, in softball and rounders, runs are scored each time a batting team member crosses the fourth base.
- In some sports points can be scored in both ways. For example, in cricket, runs can also be scored whilst the fielders return the ball.

Runs can be scored in different ways in cricket.

Combat sports

Examples include: boxing, freestyle wrestling and judo.

In these sports the primary aim is to perform an action that immediately ends the contest. This might be because:

- the opponent is physically unable to continue (a knockout in boxing)
- or because they have performed a winning move (for example, an Ippon in judo).

These sports also have scoring systems, so that a winner can be declared even without a winning action.

- The points are awarded on technique by a series of judges.
- After a certain number of rounds or bouts, the competitor with the most points wins.

In freestyle wrestling there are different ways to score points.

Throwing and jumping sports

Examples include discus, javelin, long jump and pole vault.

The aim in these sports is to throw something or jump the longest distance.

Target sports

Examples include: archery, shooting, bowls, golf and snooker.

The aim in these sports is to hit some kind of target. Points are awarded in different ways. For example:

- In sports like archery, darts and shooting, points are awarded according to the zone they hit on the target, or whether they hit the target at all.
- In sports like bowls and curling, points are awarded according to how close competitors get to the target.
- In sports like snooker and pool, the aim is to pot balls in pockets on a table. Points are associated with the balls, or given to the player who pots the most balls.
- In golf, the aim is to get the ball into the hole with the fewest number of hits. This means the player with the lowest score wins.

Races

Examples include: athletics, cycling and speed skating.

Scoring in any kind of race is simple: the aim is to finish ahead of the other competitors.

Judged sports

Examples include: rhythmic gymnastics, synchronised swimming and diving.

- Judges score each competitor against specific criteria.
- The competitors with the highest score at the end of the competition wins.

In archery different coloured rings represent different points.

What happens in a tie?

There are a number of things that can happen in the event of a tie in normal play:

- Extra time is added so that play can continue, and hopefully produce a winner. Examples include football and rugby knockout matches.
- If things are still tied then there is a 'sudden death' knockout. The most familiar example is the penalty shootout in football.
- In other sports, extra points are played for, with a 'sudden death' component. For example, in tennis a tie-break at the end of match means that one player has to reach 7 points and be 2 points clear of their opponent. If the score is 7-6 then points continue to be played until one player is 2 points ahead.
- Some sports are designed so that they cannot end in a tie. For instance, in snooker no match can ever end in a draw.
- In some sports a draw is an acceptable result. For example, in test cricket and in league games in football. In these cases, the match just ends as normal.

The longest tennis match of all time was between John Isner and Nicolas Mahut at Wimbledon in 2010. There was no tie break in the final set so the match continued for 11 hours and 5 minutes.

It took over three days! Isner won by the incredible score: 6-4, 3-6, 6-7, 7-6, 70-68

Wimbledon uses final-set tie breaks these days!

Activity

1. Describe how scoring works in:

a) squash

b) basketball

c) rounders.

Your answer should include what happens in the event of draw.

2. In each sport, what actions do the officials take to make sure the rules are followed?

Playing areas

The size of the playing area has a big effect on the way a sport is played.

When played professionally, some sports have very precisely measured playing areas, for example:

- racket sports such as badminton
- athletic events
- hockey
- lacrosse.

Other sports' playing areas have a range of acceptable sizes, for example:

- rugby league
- rugby union
- football
- cricket.

However, some parts of these playing areas are always the same size. For example:

- the width and height of the goalposts in rugby
- the location of the penalty area in football
- the size of the crease in cricket.

Intro

Choose three sport and guess the size of each playing area.

There may be other rules attached to some parts of the playing area. For example:

- In ice hockey blue lines break the rink into defensive, neutral and offensive zones. There are rules about these zones that relate to offside.
- In volleyball the attack line is set 3m back from the net. Back row players can only hit the ball over the net if they are behind, or jump from behind, the attack line.
- Goals in hockey only count if they are hit from within the penalty circle.

When played professionally, most sports' playing areas are defined. However at amateur levels these strict definitions may be relaxed.

In a few sports the exact dimensions of the playing are not important. For example:

- golf
- motor racing.

Here are playing areas from a few different sports. Can you name each sport?

Equipment

Playing equipment

Any playing equipment used in sport is regulated by the NGB. For example:

Cricket bats:

- should be made of two parts, a handle and blade
- have a maximum length and width
- have a maximum edge thickness
- must be made of wood.

Basketball:

- size 7 basketballs must weigh 624 grams, size 6 basketballs must weigh 567 grams
- size 7 basketballs must have a circumference of 74.9cm, and size 6 basketballs a circumference of 72.4cm.

Golf:

- There are specific rules about the constructions and shapes of the three categories of golf club (iron, wood and putter).
- There are also many rules about the construction of golf balls, including a minimum diameter (42.67mm) and maximum weight (45.93 grams).

Required protective equipment

Protective equipment can keep competitors safe and prevent injury. Many sports require participants to use protective equipment.

- All American football players are required to wear a helmet, to prevent head injuries.

- Batters in professional cricket are required to wear helmets, to protect their head from high-speed balls.
- A full face mask is mandatory in fencing.

Optional protective equipment

Some protective equipment does not have to be worn but is permitted by NGBs:

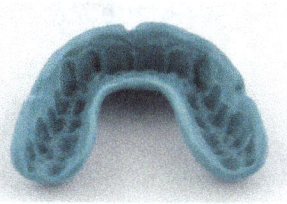

- Gum shields/mouth guards are not compulsory in rugby but they are strongly recommended for all players.
- Knee pads are optional in volleyball but are useful to prevent friction burns and bruising.
- Gloves are not mandatory for fielders in baseball but all professionals wear them because the ball moves at such high speeds.
- Shin protectors are not mandatory in hockey but are recommended.

Activity

1. a) What is the size of a football pitch?

   b) i) Name two special areas on a football pitch. ii) How big are they?

   c) How do officials make sure that the size of a football pitch follows the rules?

2. a) Name two types of protective equipment that must be warn in two different sports.

   b) Name two types of protective equipment that are optional in two different sports.

   c) How do officials in these four different sports check that rules around equipment are being followed?

B3 Starting and restarting play

Different sports have different ways to start and restart play after scoring or fouls.

Intro

Discuss how football would change if throw-ins were replaced with kick-ins.

Beginning the game

Padel	Cricket
Padel is normally played in doubles. The match, and each point after, begins with a serve. The server stands behind the baseline on the right side of the court. They aim to get the serve into the service box of the player diagonally opposite.	The captains of the teams toss a coin. The winner of the toss chooses whether to bat first or not. The batting team sends out their first two batters, who stand at either end of the pitch. The bowling team has one bowler, a wicket keeper, and a range of other fielders around the field. The match begins when the bowler delivers the first ball to one of the batters.

Fouls and infringements

Basketball	Football
Play is restarted by: - a free throw, - a throw-in from outside the playing area, - or occasionally, if it's not clear which team should have possession, a jump ball. The type of restart depends on the foul or infringement. For example: If a player is fouled whilst shooting, play is restarted by giving the fouled player free throws. The number depends as follows: - They are given two free throws if the shot didn't go in, but one free throw if it did. - If the player was attempting a 3-point shot, they are given three free throws. - If the player was attempting a 3-point shot and scored it, they are given one free throw. If the final free throw goes in then the opposing team are given a throw-in. If the final free throw does not go in then the ball is live.	Play is restarted in different ways: - Throw-ins are given if the ball goes out of play across either touchline. The throw-in is given to the team which did not touch the ball last. - Goal kicks are given if an attacking player touches the ball before it goes out of play across the defending team's goal-line. The defending team takes the goal kick. - Corners are given if a defending player touches the ball before it goes out of play across the defending team's goal-line. The attacking team can kick the ball into play from the corner of the pitch. - Free kicks are given for fouls or infringements (e.g. offside). The ball is given to the other team, who can kick the ball when it is standing still, to restart play. The opposing players must be 10 yards (9.15 metres) away from the ball. - If a foul is committed by the defending team in their own penalty area, then the attacking team is awarded a penalty. - Drop-ball. Sometimes there may be an infringement which is not either team's fault – for instance, the ball may touch the referee and interfere with play. In these cases play is restarted with an uncontested drop ball.

Restarting play after scoring

Netball	Rugby League
The teams line up in their starting positions on court. The centre from the team with the ball stands in the centre circle and attempts to throw the ball to one of their teammates in the centre third. This is called a centre pass. Each team takes it in turns to take a centre pass after a goal is scored – it doesn't matter which team scored the goal.	After scoring, the two teams line up on their sides of the pitch. The team who did not score is given a kick-off from the centre of the halfway line. The kicking team must all be behind the ball. The opposing team must be on or behind their 10-metre line. The ball must reach this 10-metre line.

How and when the game ends

Volleyball	American football
The match is played as the best of 3 or 5 sets. To win a normal set, a team must score 25 points. In the deciding set it is the first team to 15 points. In all sets, the winning team must be two points ahead of the other team. If they are not then each set continues until one team is two points ahead. The match ends when one team has won the required number of sets. The referee signals the end of the match by bringing both arms together in a cross in front of their chest, with the palms inwards.	The game is divided into four quarters of 15 minutes each. At the end of the fourth quarter the team with the most points wins. However, in the NFL, if the score is a draw, then a 10 minute period of overtime is played. There are several different scenarios that can play out in overtime but in summary: • In the regular season, there is a sudden death element in overtime. For example, if the receiving team scores a touchdown straight from kick-off then the game is over, even though the other team did not touch the ball. • If the game is still tied at the end of overtime then it is a draw. • In the playoffs, a rule change in 2021 means that both teams have a chance to touch the ball (and score) before sudden death. If there is still a tie after one overtime period then another 10-minute overtime is played, until there is a winner. These rules are for the NFL. Different competitions may tweak these rules. The referee signals the end of the game by raising one hand, or the ball, in the air.

Activity

1. a) Describe how a doubles tennis match begins. b) What actions do the officials take?

2. Describe two different infringements in a) volleyball, and b) netball.

3. Describe how play is restarted after scoring in a) football, b) badminton, and c) basketball.

4. How does play end in the following sports? a) Rugby Union, b) padel, c) World Cup football.

How officials deal with rule breaking

We have covered a range of rules for different sports. Each sport also has rules that cover:

- general play
- physical contact and general conduct

Every sport has a system in place when for what happens when these rules are broken.

Playing rules

Playing rules are in place to make the sport competitive, fun to play and entertaining to watch.

Here are some examples of playing rules and what happens when they are broken.

Wheelchair tennis

Playing rule: The ball cannot bounce more than twice before being returned.

What happens if this rule is broken? The returning player loses the point.

How do the officials communicate this to the player? It is normally quite clear that the point has been lost, so the umpire reads out the updated score.

Football

Playing rule: Outfield players cannot handle the ball.

What happens if this rule is broken? A free kick or penalty is given to the opposing team, depending on where the handball occurred. The player who handled the ball will be given a yellow card if it was deemed to be deliberate, or a red card if it prevented a clear goal-scoring opportunity.

How do the officials communicate this to the player? The referee blows their whistle, stops the game and awards the free kick. If the assistant referee spots the infringement they can alert the referee. Potential handballs in the build-up to a goal are investigated by Video Assistant Referees where they are in place.

> **Intro**
> Discuss the benefits and drawbacks of the 'sin bin'.

Basketball

Playing rule: Travelling with the ball is not allowed. (Travelling is taking steps while holding the ball.)

What happens if this rule is broken? The opposing team is given a throw-in.

How do the officials communicate this to the player? The referee uses a hand signal.

Physical contact and general conduct rules

Rugby Union

Playing rule: Players must ensure they do not cause injury to another player, either intentionally or through dangerous play (such as a high tackle).

What happens if this rule is broken? The player is given a yellow or red card. The yellow card means the player must leave the pitch for ten minutes. The red card means the player is removed from the game.

How do the officials communicate this to the player? The player is shown a yellow or red card by the referee.

Tennis

Playing rule: Players must not throw, hit or damage their racket.

What happens if this rule is broken? The player is given a first code violation. If it continues to happen they are given a second code violation and loses a point. A third code violation means they lose that game in the set.

How do the officials communicate this to the player? The umpire clearly tells the player that they have picked up a code violation, and what it is for.

Application of rules and regulations by officials

As described above, officials can use signals to communicate rule breaking to players. For example, ice hockey has a very complex set of visual signals that the officials use to communicate decisions to the players, other officials, and the general public.

In football, assistant referees use flags to show that the ball has gone out of bounds.

This handball referee is using a headset to talk to other officials. Officials in many professional sports use headsets.

Positioning

Officials need to be in the right place to see what is happening. This helps them to make the right decisions.

For example, in racket sports the line judges need to be stand in the right place to see their lines. The umpire sits in a high chair so that they can see every part of the court.

This American football referee is well positioned to see what is happening along the line of scrimmage.

Notice how the referee is near the action in this football match.

Activity

1. Describe a common playing rule in a) volleyball, and b) netball. In each case, describe what happens if this rule is broken.

2. An important playing rule in football is the offside rule. a) Explain the offside rule. b) How do officials enforce the offside rule? c) What actions and signals do officials take if a player is offside?

3. The concussion protocol is a very important procedure in rugby union. a) Describe the concussion protocol, and b) explain what the officials do as part of the protocol.

4. Describe three different ways in which a football referee can communicate to players and other officials.

C1 Planning drills and conditioned practices to develop participants' sporting skills

Drills to improve specific techniques in different sports

One way to become a better sportsperson is to improve technique and skill. **Drills** are a good way to do this and are commonly used in training.

Drills focus on particular skills, or parts of a skill, in isolated practice.

In a coach-led drill session, a coach will:

- explain the purpose of the drill
- give a demonstration of the drill
- ask the performer to perform the drill
- correct the performer's technique as needed
- ask the performer to repeat the drill a number of times.

Drills can increase in complexity, until they more closely resemble a competitive situation.

Unopposed stationary drills

These are the simplest drills. For example, a set of drills for dribbling in football might start with learning how to kick a stationary football with the insole.

> **Intro**
>
> In 1 minute list all the drills you have used in a sport of your choice.

In any sport or physical exercise there is a risk of injury. You must consider the health and safety of all participants.

You should make sure that:

- everyone carries out a warm-up before taking part
- everyone carries out a cool-down at the end of the session
- does not take part if they are feeling ill or already have an injury.

Warm-ups were covered in Component 1.

Drills with the introduction of travel

In these drills the player introduces movement.

In our example, the player runs with the ball, learning close control using the insole.

Drills with passive opposition

In these drills, elements are introduced to make things a bit more realistic.

In our example, once the player can demonstrate close control of the ball, they then have to practice moving the ball around and changing direction.

In this example the drill uses stationary cones. Other players could be used instead of cones, as long as they did not try and tackle.

Drills with active opposition

In the most advanced drills, opposition is introduced and asked to behave like they would in a real game.

In our example, players are now asked to use their close control skills to get past players who are trying to tackle.

Activity

1. a) i) List an important skill in two different sports. ii) What are the techniques involved in this skill?

    b) Can you think of a stationary drill for each skill?

    c) Can you think of a moving drill for each skill?

    d) Can you think of a drill with passive opposition for each skill?

    e) Can you think of a drill with active opposition for each skill?

2. For each drill in parts 1b)–e), explain how the drill will improve the sporting skill.

Conditioned practice

Conditioned practice is when the rules of a practice game are changed in order to focus on particular skills.

Intro
In 1 minute list the different conditioned practice you have used in a sport of your choice.

Conditioned practice allows a performer to apply skills in a more realistic setting. But the change of rules will encourage them to do things they wouldn't normally do in a real game.

Examples of conditioned practice include:

- Reduced numbers of players.
- Only allowed to score from certain zones of the pitch.
- Changes to rules about tackling, e.g. touch rugby. Touch rugby can be used to remove tackling and focus on passing and movement.

- Making all players touch the ball before returning, e.g. in seated volleyball.

- Maintaining ball possession – for example, a maximum number of touches of the ball before passing, points for number of consecutive passes, goal attempts only after a certain number of passes.
- Playing with unequal sides, e.g. 1v2 in tennis, with different points scoring for each team.

In the early 2010s, the FA reduced the size of pitches and number of players in youth football. The aim was to give players more time with the ball, to develop their technical skills. This was a form of conditioned practice.

It is no coincidence that this generation of footballers won the boys' under-17s World Cup in 2017, and in 2021 the senior England men's team reached their first major final for 44 years.

- Possession to target – passes have to be forward, extra points for scoring as a result of a sequence of forward passes, extra points for moving the ball into a marked area of the pitch.
- Allowing extra points for certain shots in tennis, volleyball etc.
- Defining they type of shots that can be used, e.g. start with an underarm serve in badminton, return with a lob, then use a smash.

As well as developing skills and techniques, conditioned practice helps with decision-making, working with teammates and tactics.

Assessment

1. a) List an important skill in two different sports. These can be the same skills as on the previous page or different skills.

b) List a conditioned practice that would help develop each skill. (There should be two examples of conditioned practice in total).

c) Describe how each conditioned practice differs from a standard game or match.

2. a) Explain how each conditioned practice in question 1 will improve each sporting skill.

b) Justify why you chose that particular conditioned practice.

3. Given your answers to 2a), can you think of another conditioned practice for each skill, that will help improve the skill?

Demonstrating techniques

When planning drills and conditioned practice, you need to think about how you will demonstrate techniques.

Intro
Discuss what you think is involved in a good demonstration of a skill.

It is important to demonstrate techniques clearly so that everyone knows what to do.

If the demonstration is not clear then participants will not perform the drill correctly. This will slow down or prevent their improvement.

Use of self or peer

You can demonstrate the technique yourself.

* The benefit of this approach is that you know that you are demonstrating the technique properly.

Alternatively, you can instruct one of the participants to perform the technique in front of everyone else:

* The benefit of this approach is that you can see if the participant has any problem in following your instructions. If they do then you can correct them as they are demonstrating. This will help prevent other participants from doing it wrong.

Whether you or a peer demonstrate, you must make sure that:

- all participants can see the demonstration
- all participants can hear the demonstration.

Teaching points

Demonstrating techniques is a form of teaching. You need to consider the most effective ways to get your points across.

Your instructions should be clear and easy to understand. You should:

- Break the technique down into different parts.
- Think about how to explain each of these different parts, so that participants do it correctly and safely.
- Use short sentences or key points for each part.
- Use simple language.

It might help to use simple charts or other props in some cases.

Activity

1. a) Give two benefits of demonstrating a drill yourself.

b) Give two benefits of using a peer to demonstrate a drill.

2. a) Why is it better to avoid using long sentences and long words when demonstrating drills?

b) Think of a drill for an important skill in a sport of your choice. Describe i) how you would break the drill into separate parts, ii) the main points you would use to explain each part to another person, and iii) how you would make sure that the drill is performed safely.

3. Demonstrate your drill in 2b) to a partner. Ask them for feedback. a) Did they understand what they were being asked to do? b) How could you improve your demonstration?

C2 Drills to improve sporting performance

Organising drills and conditioned practice

When planning drills and conditioned practice you need to think about how you will demonstrate techniques.

> **Intro**
> Discuss why you think you need to be organised to run drills and conditioned practice.

Space

For each drill or conditioned practice you need to plan how much space you will need. Some examples might include:

- Using the full playing area but with some rule changes.
- Using a small part of the normal playing area.
- Using the full playing area but with multiple smaller conditioned games or drills taking place.

Equipment

Examples of equipment that can be used in drills include:

- cones
- a range of different coloured bibs
- lots more balls than for a standard match
- stopwatch
- whistle
- other specialist equipment, such as mini hurdles, smaller goals in football or floats in swimming.

Organising participants

There are lots of ways to group participants.

- In conditioned practice, the design of the game might specify exactly how many people should take part.
- Drills can be organised in large groups, small groups or pairs.

Depending on numbers, you could have different groups working on different drills at the same time. But this requires careful planning to make sure no group is standing around waiting for other groups to finish.

Timing

A training session would normally contain a number of different drills or conditioned games. You need to plan the timing for each element to make sure:

- there is enough time for the participants to get the hang of what they are doing, and improve their technique
- that drills do not go on for too long and become boring
- that drills are not repeated too many times so that they risk injuring participants.

Demonstrating and positioning

As discussed on page 114, demonstrations should be

- easy for everyone to see and hear
- broken down into key parts
- clearly explained in simple language.

Demonstrations should be repeated a few times, to make sure that everyone can understand what you are asking them to do.

Activity

1. Think of a drill for a specific skill in a sport of your choice.

a) How much space will you need for participants to perform the drill?

b) List the equipment you will need.

c) Describe how you will organise the participants when learning and performing the drill.

d) Describe how long the drill session will take. Include time for a warm-up, demonstration, teaching, and feedback to participants.

2. Now think of a conditioned practice for the same skill. Answers questions 1a)–d) again but this time for the conditioned practice instead of the drill.

Supporting participants taking part in drills and conditioned practice

After demonstrating and explaining each drill or conditioned activity, participants will try to perform it themselves.

You need to provide help and support as they do so.

The aim of your support is to make sure that they improve their technique for each sporting skill. To do this, you will need to do the following:

- **Observe participants**: You must watch everyone carefully to make sure they perform each drill correctly.
- If anyone is not doing it correctly you may need to demonstrate it again. You may also need to provide further **instructions** and **teaching points**. Just like in the initial instruction and demonstration, instructions and teaching points should be simple, clear, and broken down.
- You should **provide feedback** to all participants.

> **Intro**
>
> Discuss what you think is meant by 'body language'.

Providing feedback

Feedback should be constructive. This means you should:

- State what participants are doing well.
- But also explain what they could do to improve.

You should always aim to encourage performers rather than just criticise.

Your feedback should always keep in mind the ultimate aim: to perform the drill properly, in order to improve the specific sporting technique.

Providing feedback is a form of communication. Communication is not just what we say, it is:

- how we say something (i.e. tone of voice)
- our facial expression
- our general body language.

Here are some examples of good and poor body language:

Activity

1. a) Explain why it is important to consider your body language when demonstrating and providing feedback to participants.

   b) Write down i) three examples of good body language and ii) three examples of poor body language.

2. How often should you provide feedback to participants during a drill?

3. To get top marks in this part of the assessment you should 'consistently provide appropriate support'.

   Explain what you think this statement means.

Component 3 Developing fitness to improve other participants' performance in sport and physical activity

In this component you will learn about:

- Fitness testing principles and measuring exercise intensity
- A range of fitness tests for different components of fitness
- Fitness training methods and their effects on body systems
- Creating successful fitness programmes

There are four learning outcomes in this component.

A Explore the importance of fitness for sports performance

- A1 The importance of fitness for successful participation in sport
- A2 Fitness training principles
- A3 Exercise intensity and how it can be determined

B Investigate fitness testing to determine fitness levels

- B1 Importance of fitness testing and requirements for administration of each fitness test
- B2 Fitness test methods for components of physical fitness
- B3 Fitness test methods for components of skill-related fitness
- B4 Interpretation of fitness test results

C Investigate different fitness training methods

- C1 Requirements for each of the following fitness training methods
- C2 Fitness training methods for physical components of fitness
- C3 Fitness training methods for skill-related components of fitness
- C4 Additional requirements for each of the fitness training methods
- C5 Provision for taking part in fitness training methods
- C6 The effects of long-term fitness training on the body systems

D Investigate fitness programming to improve fitness and sports performance

- D1 Personal information to aid training fitness programme design
- D2 Fitness programme design
- D3 Motivational techniques for fitness programming

Assessment

This component is assessed with a 1.5 hour written exam, marked and graded by the awarding body. The exam paper is taken under exam conditions. Component 3 builds on the knowledge and skills from Components 1 and 2. The exam will test your understanding across the whole qualification.

A1 The importance of fitness for successful participation in sport

Types of sport requiring specific components of fitness

In Component 2 you covered components of physical fitness and components of skill-related fitness. Different sports need different components. In team sports, different positions may need different components too.

Intro

Without looking back at your work in Component 2, list as many examples of components of fitness as you can in 1 minute.

Here are some examples.

Aerobic endurance is very important for sports or activities that last more than around 30 minutes.

For example: road cycling, long-distance running, outfield football players, especially midfielders.

Muscular endurance is also very important for sports or activities that last for more than 30 minutes.

For example, long distance races and triathlons. The examples given for aerobic endurance also need good muscular endurance.

Muscular strength is important for any sports or activities where the athlete has to create a large force.

For example, weightlifting, rowing and sprinting.

Speed is important in any sport or activity where parts of the body, or equipment, need to be moved quickly.

For example, the speed of a hockey stick, a cricket bowler's arm, or a sprinter's legs.

Speed can be important for some positions in team sports, for example wingers in football and backs in rugby.

Some **flexibility** is important in almost all sports or activities. The flexibility of different joints is more important in some events than others. For example:

- gymnasts needs a large amount of flexibility for many joints
- badminton players need good flexibility in the wrist and shoulders
- high jumpers need flexible joints in their back and neck.

Different sports and activities benefit from different **body compositions**. For example, long-distance runners and road cyclists have a very low levels of body fat. Sprinters, boxers and weightlifters have high levels of muscle mass.

Power is important in any sport or activity where a force is applied at high speed, to produce explosive movement.

For example, shot put, tennis, and triple jump.

Agility is important in any sport or activity where the performer needs to change speed or direction quickly.

For example, slalom skiing, field hockey and backs running past the opposition in rugby union.

Reaction time is important in any sport or activity where a competitor needs to react to something quickly.

For example, in any race start, or a goalkeeper saving a point-blank shot.

Balance is important in almost all sports and activities, so the performer does not fall over. It is particularly important when the base of support is very narrow, or when a performer is changing direction at high speed.

For example, in this photograph footballers are working on their balance by practising with a ball while standing on a mini-trampoline.

Coordination of two or more body parts is important in many sports and activities, and can include the movement of equipment too.

For example, performing complex actions such as the high jump, or sports where you hit a ball, such as tennis and baseball.

The player in this photograph needs to coordinate his eyes, hands, and legs in order to successfully hit the ball.

Activity

Emma plays cricket at her local club every week.

1. a) Name two components of fitness that are important in cricket.

   b) Explain why improving each component will make Emma a better cricketer.

   c) Name one other sport that needs the same two components of fitness.

125

A2 Fitness training principles

Basic principles of fitness training

There are four basic principles of fitness training. Together they are known as FITT.

- **Frequency**. This means how often the training sessions are repeated.
- **Intensity**. This means how hard each training session is.
- **Time**. This is how long each training session is.
- **Type**. This means exactly what type of training is taking place in each session

Successful training programmes use the FITT principle to make sure that:

- There is enough training each week, but not so much that it is likely to cause an injury.
- There is a mixture of easy and hard (intense) workouts.
- Training sessions last long enough to provide benefit, but not so long that they might lead to injury.
- There is a mix of different types of training across each week. For example, working on different sets of muscles during a strength-training programme.

All training plans are designed for individuals, and everyone is different. The principles of FITT will lead to different training plans for different people.

Intro

Discuss how often you think a professional tennis player trains. Do you think they do the same training every day?

Additional principles of training

In addition to FITT, training plans need to also consider the following principles:

- **Adaptation**. The human body adapts to training. For example, running for 30 minutes at a gentle pace gives the body's aerobic system a workout. When recovering from the run, physical changes in the body slightly improve its aerobic system. Continual small improvements are why training works.

- **Progressive overload**. Adaptation relies on overload. Overload means pushing the body slightly beyond what is currently comfortable. As the body adapts and gets better at the activity, the training needs to get harder to continue to overload the body. To continually improve, progressive overload means that training sessions should get harder over time.

- **Rest and recovery**. Because training relies on adaptation after being overloaded, the body needs time to recover and repair itself. It is when the body is resting that it repairs itself and improves. So rest and recovery are really important parts of a training plan.
- **Specificity**. This means that the training should be specific to the end goal.
  * For example, long-distance cyclists and long-distance runners both need good aerobic endurance. However, a training plan for runners that included cycling would not work as well as a training plan that included lots of running.
  * Similarly, a training plan for a striker in football would be different to a training plan for a defender.
- **Individual differences**. Each individual is different. To prevent injury, and obtain the right level of progressive overload, all training should be adapted for the individual.
- **Reversibility**. If there is a break in training then the body not only stops getting better, it loses performance. This is true for overall fitness, and different systems or muscles in the body too.
  * For example, if a footballer skips upper body strength workouts then their upper body will become weaker, even if they are still working hard on their aerobic fitness.
- **Variation**. It is important that performers are motivated to train. A variety of exercises in training sessions can help with motivation and stop performers becoming bored. This is important because boredom can lead to missed training sessions, which reverses any gains.

Activity

Joshua is training for the London marathon. His training plan includes a long run at an easy pace at the weekend. In the first week of the plan the long run is for 10km, but it increases by 1km each week.

1. State two additional principles of training present in this part of his plan.
2. a) State which FITT principle 'an easy pace' represents.
   b) Name one other FITT principle in this part of his plan.

A3 Exercise intensity

Intensity

Intensity is how hard the training is. Different training sessions are run at different intensities.

Training at the right intensity is very important. Heart rate gives us a good idea of how intensely we are exercising.

Intro

Estimate your resting heart rate and write it down. After reading this page you can measure your heart rate and compare it to your guess.

Heart rate and training zones

Measuring heart rate

You can measure your heart rate at your wrist or neck.

- Place your index finger and middle finger against your neck or wrist until you find your pulse.
- Set a timer for one minute and count how many beats you feel. Alternatively, you can count for 30 seconds and then multiply the result by 2.
- Do not use your thumb to measure pulse, as it has its own pulse which will confuse your readings.

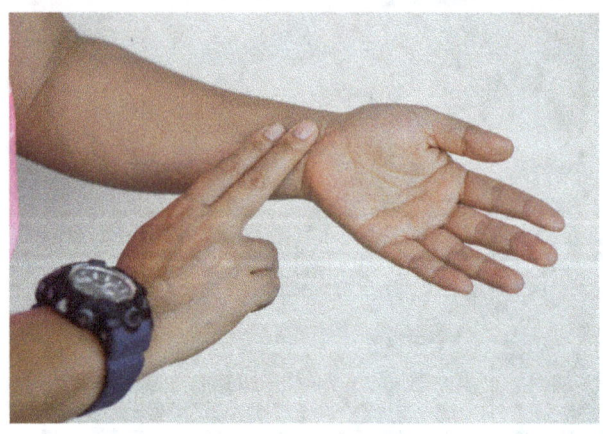

Maximum heart rate

To use heart rate to estimate intensity, we also need to know the maximum heart rate (HR Max).

Heart rate is measured in beats per minute (bpm). HR Max is the maximum number of beats per minute for an individual.

Each person's HR Max is different. But we can estimate HR Max as follows:

$$\text{HR Max} = 220 - (\text{person's age})$$

For example, a 14 year old's estimated HR Max is: 220 - 14 = 206 bpm

Note: This formula provides an estimate. However every individual is different and their actual HR Max is likely to be a little different.

Training zones

When people exercise their heart rate increases. We can express heart rate during exercise as a percentage of HR Max. The percentage shows how intense the exercise is.

The percentage of HR Max is broken down into training zones. Training in different zones does different things.

Zone 1 Very light
Warm-up and cool-down
50-60% HR Max

Zone 2 Light
Fat-burning zone
60-70% HR Max

Zone 3 Moderate
Aerobic zone
70-80% HR Max

Zone 4 Hard
Anaerobic zone
Over 80% HR Max

Training in Zone 2 (Fat Burning Zone 60-70%) is good for training the body to use stored fat as an energy source. You should be able to exercise for a long time in this zone.

Training in Zone 3 (Aerobic Zone 70-80% of HR Max) is good for developing aerobic endurance.

Training in Zone 4 (Anaerobic Zone over 80% of HR Max) will develop the anaerobic energy system. This is a special system which provides energy without using oxygen. It is used during short, intense activities such as a 100m sprint.

Training plans normally contain sessions each week that focus on a different training zone.

Note: Training in the anaerobic zone (Zone 4) means that heart rate is getting close to its maximum. This places stress on the heart and is potentially very dangerous for people who are not fit.

For example, a 20 year old has a HR Max of 220-20 = 200 bpm. After 5 minutes of a training session they measure their heart rate as 120 bpm. As a percentage of HR Max, this is:

100% × 120/200 = 60%.

This is Zone 2 – the fat-burning zone.

After another 5 minutes they measure their rate as 180 bpm. As a percentage of HR Max this is:

100% × 180/200 = 90%.

This is: Zone 4 – the anaerobic zone.

Activity

Tiara has joined a rowing club. She wants to know how hard she should be training. In her first training session she measures her heart rate at 150 bpm. Tiara's HR Max is 200.

1. a) Which zone was Tiara training in during this session?

b) State which component of fitness this zone is good for.

c) Explain if this training session will improve Tiara's performance as a rower.

Borg Rating of Perceived Exertion Scale

Another way to measure intensity of exercise is to ask people how hard the training feels. Asking people how hard it feels is called their **perceived exertion**.

We can use a rating system for people to categorise how hard the activity feels.

- The lowest rating is 6, which is when we are at rest and our heart rate is normal.
- The highest rating is 20, when we are at the maximum possible exertion.

Intro
Walk up and down a flight of stairs twice. How hard did it feel?

Perceived Exertion	Description
6 No exertion	At rest.
7-8 Extremely light	E.g. gentle yoga.
9-10 Very light	Walking at comfortable pace. Very easy to talk normally.
11-12 Light	Breathing is deeper but still able to hold a conversation.
13-14 Somewhat hard	Can only say a few words at a time.
15-16 Hard	Breathing is deep and hard. Talking is very hard.
17-18 Very hard	Very uncomfortable. A healthy person can continue at this level for a little while but they are pushing themselves to their limit.
19 Extremely hard	This is the greatest exertion that most people will ever feel.
20 Maximum exertion	

This rating system is called the Borg Rating of Perceived Exertion (RPE) Scale. (Borg was the name of the scientist who came up with it.)

We can convert the Borg RPE rating to a heart rate estimate as follows:

Heart rate (in bpm) = Borg rating × 10

For example, if a 40-year-old woman rates their training as '12 – Light', then her heart rate is estimated as:

Heart rate = 12 × 10

= 120 bpm.

The maximum heart rate for a 40-year-old woman is estimated as:

220 − 40 = 180 bpm

We can work out her percentage of HR Max as:

100% × 120/180 = 67%.

67% of HR Max is Zone 2 – the fat-burning zone.

Technology for measuring intensity

Taking a pulse is a good way to measure heart rate. However, it can be difficult to take a pulse whilst exercising.

Technology provides some other ways to measure heart rate.

Heart-rate monitors are special straps that fit around the chest and detect heart rate. They send their data to a running watch. The athlete can check their pulse, and how it changes, on the watch as they train.

Some smartwatches have a heart-rate monitor built into them. They detect the pulse at the wrist.

There are also apps for smartphones that can measure heart rate directly. They do this by measuring the light reflected from your finger. This changes during each pulse.

Other apps are also designed to communicate with running watches, heart-rate monitor straps and smart watches. This means that heart-rate data collected during training can be analysed later.

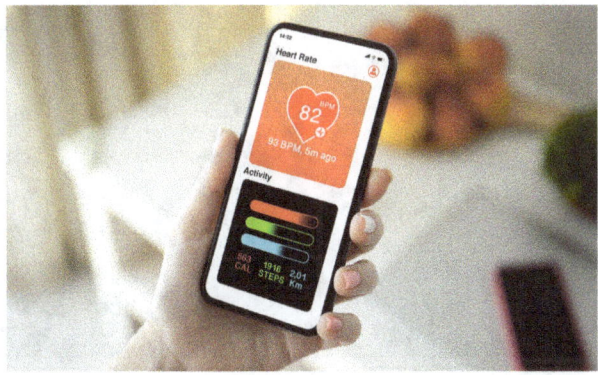

Activity

Marley is a swimmer who would like to estimate his training zone during a training swim.

1. Describe how Marley can use the Borg scale to estimate his training zone.

2. Marley receives some money for his birthday and decides to buy some technology to measure intensity. Describe the different options Marley could spend his money on.

3. Assess the most appropriate method for Marley to work out his training zone.

4. Handa is a long-distance runner with an HR Max of 200 bpm. Her Borg rating is 15 during a training session. Identify which of the following is her likely heart rate:

A: 50 bpm **B**: 100 bpm **C**: 150 bpm **D**: 200 bpm

A3

Repetition max

1RM

For muscular strength training we need another way to measure intensity.

1RM is called the one repetition max. It is the heaviest weight a person can lift for just one time. 1RM is measured in kilograms (kg).

1RM is 100% intensity for muscular strength.

Once we know the 1RM weight we can work out what weights are needed to work at a lower intensity for muscular strength:

Weight they should lift = 1RM × intensity

Intro

Discuss which exercise for which you are likely to have the highest 1RM

For example, Elina's 1RM for a bench press is 60kg.

To work at 70% intensity for muscular strength:

Weight she should lift = 60 × 70/100

= 42kg

To work at 85% intensity:

Weight she should lift = 60 × 85/100

= 51 kg

Muscular strength training uses **high intensity** and **low repetitions**.

15RM

For muscular endurance training we need a different way to measure intensity.

15RM is the maximum weight that someone can lift 15 times in a row. 15RM is measured in kilograms (kg).

15RM is 100% intensity for muscular endurance.

Once we know the 15RM weight we can work out what weights are needed to work at a lower intensity for muscular endurance:

Weight they should lift = 15RM × intensity

For example, Mark's 15RM for a bench press is 40kg.

To work at 60% intensity for muscular endurance:

Weight he should lift = 40 × 60/100

= 24kg

Muscular endurance training uses **low intensity** and **high repetitions**.

Activity

1. Identify which **one** of these statements is true:

A: 1RM is a way to measure maximum muscular endurance.

B: A 15RM bench press is the most important test for a marathon runner.

C: A shot putter could use a 1RM shoulder press as part of his strength training.

D: 15RM is normally larger than 1RM.

Sally is a javelin thrower. Her 1RM shoulder press is 50kg. She wants to train for muscular strength at 80% intensity. Identify which weight she should lift:

A: 40kg **B:** 45kg **C:** 8kg **D:** 48kg

B1 Importance of fitness testing

Reasons for fitness testing

Baseline data

Fitness testing at the start of the training plan provides **baseline data.**

Baseline data are the scores and results from the first fitness tests.

They show the performer's level before training began.

These results are used to design the training plan so it is as effective as possible for the individual.

Design training programmes

The results of fitness tests show what a performer is already good at, and what they need to improve.

Is training working?

Fitness testing throughout the training plan shows whether the plan is working.

For example, testing can check if a distance runner's aerobic endurance is getting better. If it is not improving fast enough, then the plan can be changed.

Goal-setting aims

Fitness testing allow goals to be very specific.

For example, instead of simply 'getting better at sprinting' a winger in rugby can aim to improve their 30m sprint test results by 0.2 seconds.

Something to aim for

Having a specific goal helps with a performer's motivation.

Knowing that there will be a test in a few weeks can motivate a performer to put their maximum effort into every session.

Meeting goals or showing improvement can also be very motivating for performers, who often like the competition with themselves.

Pre-test procedures

There are several things that need to be done before a fitness test can begin.

Calibrate equipment

For a fitness test to be useful it has to give accurate results.

To do this, fitness test equipment must be **calibrated**. This means that:

- Equipment must be set to measure zero at the start of a test e.g. stopwatches should be reset, measuring equipment should be placed in the correct starting place.
- Measurements can be compared with known quantities, e.g. comparing scale readings with a known weight.
- Results should be compared with other similar equipment that measures the same thing. If there are any significant differences in readings then further investigation is needed.

Informed consent

Participants need to sign an **informed consent** form. Informed consent means that the participant:

- understands exactly what they will be asked to do in the test
- understands that they need to follow all instructions
- understands the risks involved
- with all this in mind agrees to take part the test, and to follow all instructions and health and safety rules.

A consent form is dated and signed by the participant and the person carrying out the test before the test begins.

PAR-Q

PAR-Q stands for Physical Activity Readiness Questionnaire. This questionnaire must be completed before any training or exercise.

It asks a series of questions about a person's medical history. It also asks if they have any fitness or injury problems that might affect their ability to exercise.

If the PAR-Q reveals any problems then the participant is advised to speak to a doctor before undertaking any exercise.

The PAR-Q is used because exercise can be dangerous for people with certain conditions.

There is no standard format for a PAR-Q but there is an example on the next page.

PAR-Q Form

1. Has your doctor ever recommended that you only do physical activity recommended by a doctor?

2. Do you have a heart condition?

3. Have you ever had chest pain during or after exercise?

4. Do you ever feel faint or have severe dizziness?

5. Do you have high blood pressure?

6. Has your doctor ever said that you have a bone or joint problem which may be made worse by exercise?

7. Do you have any pain or problems with your back?

8. Are you currently taking any prescribed medication?

9. Do you have asthma or have breathing problems?

10. Have you given birth in the last six months?

11. Are you pregnant?

12 Have you had surgery in the last year?

12. Do you know of any reason why you should not exercise?

Name:
Signature:
Date:

Pre-fitness check

Before undertaking any training, the trainer needs to understand the general level of fitness of the participant. A pre-fitness check allows the trainer to check:

- Lifestyle – such as whether they smoke, drink alcohol, have a good diet.
- Their current levels of activity – how much exercise, and what type of exercise, each week.
- That they have not done any exercise the same day as the test.
- That they have not just eaten.
- That they are wearing appropriate clothes and shoes for the test.
- Double-check that the details on the PAR-Q form have not changed since it was completed.

Administrating fitness tests

Before running a fitness test

Before running a fitness test you need to:
- know what tests are available
- understand the standard methods to run each test
- know what equipment is needed for each test.

These details are included in the descriptions about a range of standard fitness tests, in sections B2 and B3.

Selecting a fitness test

You will need to choose the most appropriate fitness test. Selecting the right test depends on:
- the individual performer's fitness and abilities
- the performer's chosen sport or activity
- the component of fitness that the session is investigating.

During the fitness test

During the fitness test you will need to accurately measure and record the test results.
- Carefully take a reading at the right time if you are using equipment (e.g. a stopwatch).
- You must write down each result as soon as you take a reading.
- You should use the correct units for each reading, as explained in the test methods. For example, is distance measured in feet or metres?

After the fitness test

After the test you will need to interpret the results. This is so you and the performer can understand what they mean.

Results can be interpreted using data tables. These describe what the results mean for different genders and ages. Details of the correct data tables are included in sections B2 and B3 and from page 208.

> **Activity**
>
> Jana has joined a private gym. The gym wants to conduct some fitness tests with Jana.
>
> 1. Describe **three** reasons why fitness testing is important.
>
> 2. Match the terms on the left with the correct definitions on the right:
>
> A: PAR-Q
>
> B: Calibration
>
> C: Pre-fitness test
>
> D Informed Consent
>
> 1: Used to check lifestyle and fitness
>
> 2: Used to check medical conditions
>
> 3: Used to confirm participants understand what they are doing
>
> 4: Used to ensure test will give correct results

B1 Reliability, validity and practicality of fitness tests

Reliability

A test is **reliable** if it can be repeated many times and still give the same result.

Reliability is affected by:

- **Calibration** of equipment: if equipment is not calibrated it will give incorrect results. If the test is repeated using different equipment, it would give different results.
- **Motivation** of the participant: fitness tests assume that participants are trying their hardest. If they are not then the results will not be accurate.
- The test procedure: if the standard test procedures **have** not been followed precisely then results may not be accurate.
- **Conditions**: Temperature, wind and altitude can all affect performance:
    * A headwind slows people down whilst tailwinds speed them up – wind is only a factor outdoors.
    * Warm conditions can hinder aerobic performance – this is true both indoors and outdoors.
    * High altitude affects aerobic performance because there is less oxygen in the air – this is true both indoors and outdoors.

Motivation: If someone runs an aerobic endurance test slower than they are able to, then the result will not describe their true aerobic endurance.

- Experience of the person running the test: a less experienced person is more likely to overlook one of the other factors listed here.

Validity

Validity is deciding what conclusions can be taken from the results of a test.

For example, a good score in a press-up test does not mean you can assume the person has good muscular endurance in their legs. This is because the press-up mainly tests the upper body.

This means that the press-up test is not a valid test to assess muscular endurance of long-distance cyclists.

Practicality

When choosing a test you need to consider how **practical** it is. This depends on the aim of the session. For example, some fitness tests used for professional athletes are not practical for an amateur.

Practicality depends on:

- **Cost**: hiring equipment, people or venues can be costly.
- **Time** to set up and perform the test: if there is limited time then some tests may be ruled out because they take too long to set up, or too long to run.
- **Time** to analyse data: a complex test, with many measurements, will collect a lot of data to analyse. Taking time to analyse large amounts of data may be appropriate for a Premier League football team, where they are looking for a tiny gain in performance. But it is not practical for someone playing Sunday League football.

Elite fitness tests use expensive equipment and people.

- **Number of participants at one time**: some tests can be run for lots of people at the same time. These tests are more practical when there are a number of participants.

For example, a school rugby coach may have two or three teams to test – that's at least 45 people. If she tested them all individually it could take all day! But if she ran one group test it might take only 10-20 minutes.

Fitness tests can create a lot of data to analyse

Activity

Jana attends the fitness test at her gym. However she had a difficult day at work and does not feel motivated. Before the test, the people at the gym calibrate the equipment Jana will use.

1. Explain why Jana's motivation would affect the reliability of Jana's fitness test.
2. Explain why the equipment is calibrated before the test.
3. Jana would like to increase her upper body strength. Identify which of these is a valid test for her:

A: Aerobic endurance test **B**: Muscular endurance test **C**: Muscular strength test

B2 Fitness tests – aerobic endurance

Multistage fitness test (MSFT)

This test is a way to measure and compare aerobic endurance. Performers have to continually run 20m in time with the beeps. (For this reason it is also known as the Beep Test.)

Equipment and people
- Flat non-slip running surface of at least 25 metres
- Multistage fitness test audio (app or YouTube recording)
- Cones
- Measuring tape
- Loudspeaker
- At least one assistant, so there is one person at each row of cones. More needed with larger groups of participants.

Interpreting results
Normative data is on p.208.

Units: An entry such as 4.7 means Level 4, Shuttle 7.

Standard test method
- Set two lines of cones 20 metres apart
- After a warm-up, participants line up next to one row of cones.
- Upon the first beep they run towards the second line of cones. They aim to reach the line before the second beep.
- At the second beep they turn around and run back towards the first line of cones, before the third beep.
- Participants continue running back and forth, aiming to reach the cones before the next beep. If they reach the cones before the beep, they cannot begin their next run until the beep sounds.
- After each minute a double or triple beep shows that the level has changed. The time between beeps is shorter at each higher level. There are 23 levels in total.
- If a beep sounds before reaching the next cones, the participant is given a warning. If they get two warnings in a row then they are out. Their level, and the number of shuttle runs they complete in that level, are recorded e.g. Level 5 Shuttle 3 (L5 S3 or 5.3).
- Each participant continues until they are exhausted and unable to continue.

Reliability
Weather conditions can affect results. Ideally the test would be run indoors, or in cool conditions with no wind.

This is a maximal test. If participants drop out before they are exhausted their results will not be correct.

Practicality
✓ Cheap to run – not much equipment or space

✓ Can run with larger groups

✗ Need more assistants with larger groups

Validity
Valid for aerobic endurance in sports with continual running (e.g. 10 000 metre track event).

Less valid for non-running (e.g. cycling).

Less valid for sports with intermittent running (e.g. field hockey, football, rugby).

Yo-Yo test

This test is a variation of the MSFT. It adds in short recovery periods. This makes it a more valid test for aerobic endurance in sports with breaks in running.

Equipment and people
- Flat non-slip running surface of at least 25 metres
- Yo-Yo test audio (app or YouTube recording)
- Cones
- Measuring tape
- Loudspeaker
- At least one assistant, so there is one person at each row of cones. More needed with larger groups of participants.

Interpreting results
Normative data is on p.208.
Units: An entry such as 14.8 means Level 14, Shuttle 8.

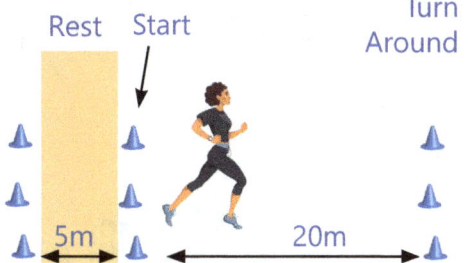

Standard test method
- Set two lines of cones as in the MSFT. Add a third set of cones another 5 metres away.
- After a warm-up, participants line up next to the Start cones.
- Upon the first beep they run towards the Turn Around cones. They aim to reach them before the second beep.
- At the second beep they turn around and run back towards the Start cones, before the third beep.
- At the third beep there is a 10-second recovery period. Participants can walk or jog in the recovery area. But they must be back at the Start cones before the next beep. Two shuttles and a recovery is called a circuit.
- After a certain number of circuits, a double or triple beep shows that the level has changed. The time between beeps is shorter at each higher level.
- If a participant misses two beeps in a row then they are out. Their level, and the number of shuttle runs they completed in that level, are recorded e.g. Level 5 Shuttle 3 (L12 S4 or 12.4).
- Each participant continues until they are exhausted and unable to continue.

Reliability
Weather conditions can affect results. Ideally the test would be run indoors, or in cool conditions with no wind.

This is a maximal test. If participants drop out before they are exhausted their results will not be correct.

Practicality
✓ Cheap to run
✓ Can run with larger groups
✗ Need more assistants with larger groups

Validity
Valid for aerobic endurance in sports with intermittent running (e.g. field hockey, football, rugby).

Less valid for sports with continual running.

Less valid for non-running sports (e.g. swimming).

Harvard step test

This test measures aerobic endurance. It is submaximal – participants do not have to put in their maximum effort to complete it.

Equipment and people
- A step or bench – 50.8cm high for men, 40cm high for women.
- Metronome
- Stopwatch or timer

The test was developed in 1942. There are many different versions of the test using different bench heights.

Interpreting results
Normative data are on p.208 onwards.

Units: number of heartbeats.

Standard test method
- The participant warms up but then rests until their heart rate is back to normal.
- The metronome is set to sound once every two seconds.
- The tester gives a countdown and then starts the timer and metronome.
- The participant is asked to step up and step down, every two seconds in time with the metronome. This means there should be 30 steps every minute.
- The tester stops the test after 5 minutes, in which time there will be 150 steps. The participant sits down.
- The tester or participant counts the **total number** of heartbeats:
    * between 1 and 1½ minutes after the end of the test
    * between 2 and 2½ minutes after the end of the test
    * between 3 and 3½ minutes after the end of the test
- A score for each participant is calculated as follows:

    Score = 30 000 / (2 × total number of heartbeats)

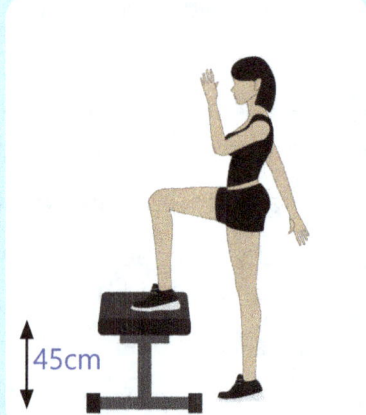

Reliability
The metronome must be calibrated to exactly two seconds.

The heart rate must be measured at the precise times described.

Test must last for 5 minutes.

Practicality
✓ Cheap to run – not much equipment or space

✓ Can run with larger groups

✗ Need more benches or steps with larger groups

Validity
The test is a good predictor of aerobic endurance.

It does not account for different heights and weights. Taller or lighter people are likely to get a better test score, even if their aerobic endurance is the same as smaller or heavier people.

There are lots of different versions of the test, often with different bench heights. You MUST make sure you choose the correct normative data for the test you have run.

12 minute Cooper test

This test measures aerobic endurance. Participants are asked to run or swim as far as they can in 12 minutes.

This is a maximal test.

Equipment and people
- Stopwatch or timer
- Whistle
- Athletics track for the running test – although any flat surface can be used if it has been accurately measured
- Swimming pool for the swimming test
- Cones
- Measuring tape

Interpreting results
Normative data on p.208 onwards.

Units: metres

Standard test method
- Whilst participants warm up, the tester uses the cones to mark out intervals on the track or pool. (Note: some tracks already have markings that can help with measurements).
- Participants are given instructions about the test. As the aim is to run or swim as far as possible in 12 minutes, they will need to pace themselves, particularly at the start.
- Using the whistle to start and stop the test, participants are timed for 12 minutes. They must stop immediately on the whistle.
- Testers count the number of laps or lengths for each participant.
- Testers use the cones and tape measure to see how far participants reached on their final lap or length. They use this and the total number of laps or lengths to calculate the total distance for each participant.

Reliability
Pacing is key for maximum distance. Inexperienced runners or swimmers are likely to get their pace wrong.

Motivation plays a large role too.

For more experienced and motivated runners and swimmers, reliability is good.

Temperature, wind and altitude have a large impact on outdoor running.

Practicality
✓ Can be cheap to run – not much equipment or space

✓ Can test a lot of participants at the same time

✗ With a lot of participants, you rely on them tracking their own laps/lengths

✗ Ideally need to use a running track

Validity
A good indicator of aerobic endurance for runners and swimmers.

Test is only valid when participants put in their maximum effort.

B2 Fitness tests – muscular endurance

One-minute press-up

This test is used to measure muscular endurance in the upper body.

Equipment and people
- Flat non-slip surface or exercise mat
- Stopwatch or timer

Interpreting results
Normative data on p.208 onwards.

Units: number of press-ups

Standard test method
- The aim of the test is to perform as many press-ups as possible in one minute.
- The participant warms up and then starts in the 'up' position, with the arms straight.
- The tester begins the test and times one minute.
- Keeping their legs and back straight, the participant lowers themselves to the ground until their elbows are at 90°. Then they raise themselves back to the starting position.
- The tester counts the number of press-ups during the test.
- People with lower upper body strength can use a modified press-up instead, where their knees are on the floor.

Press-up

Modified press-up

Reliability
Participants need to give maximum effort.

Press-up technique must be correct.

Practicality
✓ Cheap and easy to run – not much equipment or space

✓ Can run with large groups

Validity
Valid for upper body muscular endurance.

Valid for sports such as rowing, climbing and freestyle wrestling.

One-minute sit-up

This test measures the endurance of the abdominal muscles.

Equipment and people
- Flat non-slip surface or exercise mat
- Stopwatch or timer

Interpreting results
Normative data on p.208 onwards.

Units: number of sit-ups

Standard test method
- The aim of the test is to perform as many sit-ups as possible in one minute.
- The participant warms up and then lies on the floor:
    * Knees should be bent at around 90°.
    * Feet should be flat on the floor.
    * Hands should be resting on the chest or legs.
- The tester begins the test and times one minute.
- The participant engages their abdominal muscles and uses them to raise themselves off the floor until they are sat up. They should use the same muscles to gently lower themselves back to the starting position.
- The tester counts the number of sit-ups during the test.

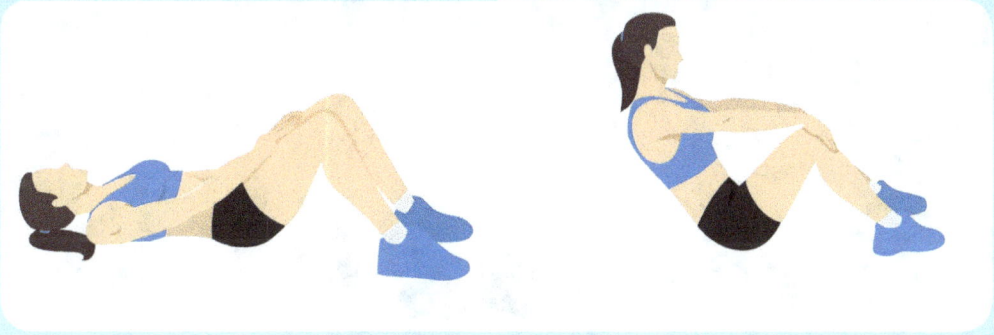

Reliability
Participants need to give maximum effort.

Sit-up technique must be correct.

Practicality
✓ Cheap and easy to run – not much equipment or space

✓ Can run with large groups

Validity
Valid for abdominal muscular endurance.

Core strength is important in many sports, but particularly sports such as gymnastics, judo and rugby.

Timed plank test

This test is used to measure muscular endurance in the upper body.

It is a maximal test – participants continue until they are not physically able to.

Equipment and people
- Flat non-slip surface or exercise mat
- Stopwatch or timer

Interpreting results
Normative data on p.208 onwards.

Units: seconds

Standard test method
- The aim of the test is to hold the plank position for as long as possible.
- Participants warm up and then take up the plank position:
    * forearms lie flat on the ground
    * legs are raised off the ground
    * only the toes and forearms are in contact with the ground
    * there should be a straight line running across the legs and back.
- Once in the correct position, the stopwatch is started.
- The participant is timed for as long as they hold the plank.

Reliability
Participants need to give their maximum effort.

Plank technique must be correct.

Practicality
✓ Cheap and easy to run – not much equipment or space

✓ Can run with large groups

Validity
Valid for abdominal muscular endurance.

Core strength is important in many sports.

B2 Fitness tests – flexibility

Sit and reach test

This test measures the flexibility of the lower back muscles and hamstrings.

Equipment and people
- Flat non-slip surface or exercise mat
- Sit and reach box

Interpreting results
Normative data on p.208 onwards.

Units: cm

Standard test method
- The aim of the test is to reach as far forward as possible. The reach should not be a jerky lunge, as this may cause injury.
- The participant warms up and removes their shoes.
- They sit with their legs stretched out so their feet are touching the box.
- They then slowly and gently reach their fingertips forward, sliding their hands across the top of the box.
- The tester records the distance their longest finger reaches, using the ruler on the box.

Reliability
Participants need to give maximum effort.

Practicality
✓ Easy to run – not much equipment or space

✗ Need a sit and reach box to run the test

✗ Not practical to run with large groups

Validity
Valid to measure lower back and hamstring flexibility. This is particularly important in sports such as gymnastics, high jump, pole vault and hurdles.

Calf muscle flexibility test

This test measures the flexibility of the calf muscles.

Equipment and people
- A wall
- A ruler or tape measure

Interpreting results
There is no normative data for this because everyone's legs are a different size. This test is best used to monitor changes in flexibility over time.

Units: cm

Standard test method
- The participant warms up.
- The tester places the ruler or tape measure on the floor, against the wall.
- The participant stands very near to a wall, with one leg in front of the other. Both feet should point to the wall.
- The participant bends their front leg at the knee, until the knee touches the wall. They must keep their front heel on the ground.
- The tester measures how far the toes are from the wall.
- The participant moves a bit further back from the wall and tries to touch the wall with their knee again.
- They keep on moving back and repeating, until they can no longer touch the wall with their knee.
- The tester notes the furthest distance the participant got from the wall while still able to touch their knee against it.
- The whole exercise is repeated for the other leg.

Reliability
This is a very reliable test if the participant follows the instructions closely.

Practicality
✓ Very cheap and easy to run — not much equipment or space
✓ Can run with larger groups

Validity
As there are no normative data, the results of this test do not accurately predict how flexible someone is.

However, repeating the test for individuals over a period of time does give a valid indication of changes in calf flexibility. Calf flexibility is important for sports such as basketball, high jump and running, and activities such as dance and yoga.

This test is not valid for flexibility of other parts of the body.

Shoulder flexibility test

This test measures flexibility of the shoulders.

Equipment and people
- Stick or rope
- Measuring tape

Interpreting results
Normative data on p.208 onwards. See below for more details.

Units: cm

Standard test method
- Ask participants to warm up.
- Participants hold a stick or rope in front of their body. Their hands can be close together and both palms should face down.
- They lift the stick or rope over their head and behind their shoulders.
- As it goes behind them, they will have to start moving their hands further apart.
- They should continue until the stick or rope is at the bottom of their back.
- The tester measures the distance between the two thumbs of the hands.
- The test can be repeated several times. The smallest distance is the best result.

Optional
- The tester can also measure the width of the shoulders.
- The tester then subtracts shoulder width from the best score in the test.

See Validity box for more about this second part of the test.

Reliability
This is a very reliable test if the participant follows the instructions closely.

Practicality
✓ Very cheap and easy to run – not much equipment or space
✓ Can run with larger groups

Validity

There are no normative data for the first part of this test. This is because the distance between the hands depends on length of arms and size of person. So the results of the first part of the test do not accurately predict how flexible someone is.

However, repeating the test for individuals over a period of time does give a valid indication of changes in shoulder flexibility. Shoulder flexibility is important for all throwing and racket sports.

The second part of the test, which subtracts shoulder length from the score, does have some normative data available. However the data was from 200 university students in 1977. Care should be taken in assuming this small sample data represents other age groups.

This test is not valid for flexibility of other parts of the body.

B2 Fitness tests – speed

30 metre sprint test

This test is used to measure acceleration and maximum running speed.

Interpreting results

Normative data on p.208 onwards. **Units**: seconds

Equipment and people

- Tape measure
- Cones
- Whistle or starter gun
- Flat surface with at least 50m of space
- Stopwatch or timer

Standard test method

- The aim of the test is to run as fast as possible.
- The tester measures a 30 metre straight line, and arranges cones at the start and end.
- The participant warms up and then lines up at the start. They should be completely stationary.
- Upon hearing the whistle or starter gun, the participant sprints as fast as they can to the end. The tester starts the stopwatch at the same time.
- The tester stops the stopwatch as the participant reaches the end cones.
- The test can be repeated two more times and the shortest time used as the final result. There should be a full recovery in between tests – preferably at least 5 minutes.

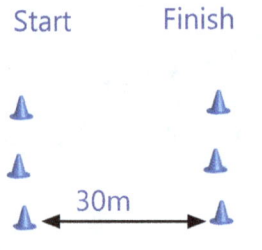

Reliability

Participants need to give maximum effort.

If outside, wind can have a big impact on results

Running surface has a big impact e.g. grass versus a running track.

Some people will be more accurate at timing than others. For a more reliable result timing gates can be used.

Practicality

✓ Cheap and easy to run (if using stopwatch) – not much equipment needed

✗ Can only run for one person at a time

✗ More expensive if using timing gates

Validity

Valid for any sports that need short bursts of fast running from a standing start e.g. rugby

Valid for sprinters, to predict the opening part of the race. But not as valid to predict performance later in a race, e.g. final 30m in a 100m race.

30 metre flying sprint test

This test measures the endurance of the abdominal muscles.

Equipment and people
- Tape measure
- Cones
- Whistle or starter gun
- Flat surface with at least 70m of space
- Stopwatch or timer

Interpreting results
Normative data on p.208 onwards.

Units: seconds

Standard test method
- This test is a variation of the 30 metre sprint. The only difference is that a new finish line is laid out, 30m after the previous finish line. The old finish line becomes the timing line. This is so participants hit top speed before they reach the timing line.
- The participant starts from the new start line. The flying sprint is measured from the timing line until the end.
- The two tests can be combined if performers are timed from the start line – the first 30 metres are the sprint test and the last 30 metres the flying sprint test.

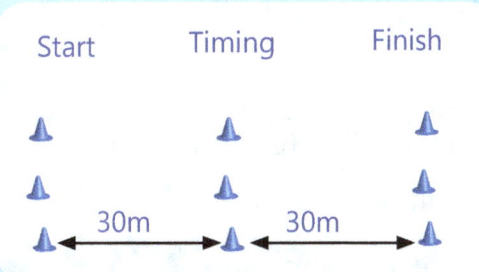

Reliability
Participants need to give maximum effort.

If outside, wind can have a big impact on results

Participants must fully recover before attempting the test again.

Some people will be more accurate at timing than others. For a more reliable result timing gates can be used.

Practicality
✓ Cheap and easy to run (if using stopwatch) – not much equipment needed

✗ Can only run for one person at a time

✗ More expensive if using timing gates

Validity
Valid to predict top speed in any sports that need short bursts of fast running e.g. football

Valid for sprinters, to predict their top speed. But not as valid to predict performance later in a race, as they begin to tire out, e.g. last 100m in a 200m race.

B2 Fitness tests – muscular strength

Grip dynamometer

This test is used to measure muscular strength of the hand and forearm.

Equipment and people
- A handgrip dynamometer

Interpreting results

Normative data on p.208 onwards.

Units: kilogram (kg) (Note: grip dynamometers tell you how many kg of mass would be needed to produce the force it measures).

Standard test method

The aim of the test is to grip the dynamometer as hard as possible.

- The test starts with the dominant hand. The handle is adjusted to fit the participant's hand size.
- The participant should sit down, with feet flat on the floor.
- The elbow is bent at a right angle with the dynamometer held out.
- The participant is asked to squeeze the handle as hard as they can for 3 seconds.
- The arm should not move when performing the test.
- The reading is noted.
- The test is repeated two more times on the same hand, and the best of the three results recorded. Care is taken to record which hand the test was for.
- The test is repeated on the other hand.

Reliability

The dynamometer must be calibrated before use.

The handle must be adjusted to fit each participant's hand.

Practicality

✓ Easy to run the test
✗ Needs specialist equipment
✗ Not cheap

Validity

Valid to predict hand and forearm strength.

Valid for racket sports and throwing sports, and sports such as climbing and weightlifting.

One rep max (1RM) test

This test measures muscular strength of any muscle group.

Equipment and people
- Free weights or weight machine
- Weighing scales
- A second person is needed to 'spot' – help get weights in place and for safety reasons if the weight is too much for the participant

Interpreting results
Normative data on p.208 onwards.

Units: kg

Standard test method

The aim of the test is to find out the heaviest weight that a muscle group can lift. Each muscle group uses a different technique or machine but the general method is:

- The participant warms up and then lies on the floor.
- The tester and participant choose a weight that should be easily achievable. The participant lifts this weight once.
- The participant rests for several minutes.
- A slightly heavier weight is chosen and the test is repeated.
- The participant rests again for several minutes.
- This continues until the participant reaches a weight that they cannot lift. The tester should note down all of the weights achieved as the participant lifts them. The heaviest weight is the 1RM for that muscle group.

Popular 1RM exercises, and the muscles they test, include:

- chest press for pectorals
- lat pull down for latissimus dorsi
- bicep curl for biceps
- shoulder press for deltoids
- leg extension for quadriceps
- leg curl for hamstrings.

The score can be used to track individual progress. But to compare to other people, you can calculate a score relative to body weight:

Relative strength = 1RM weight (kg) / body mass (kg)

Reliability
Exactly the same test procedure should be followed for each test.

1RM tests should only be undertaken on indoor equipment in excellent condition.

Practicality
× Needs specialist equipment
× Testers should be experienced
× Participants should also have some experience of lifting weights
× Only one person can be tested at a time

Validity
In general each test is valid as a measure of muscular strength for the given muscles. However you should check that there is normative data for the age group that is being tested.

Muscular strength is important in many sports, including rugby, weightlifting, gymnastics and rowing.

B2 Fitness tests – body composition

Body Mass Index (BMI)

This test is used as a way to estimate body composition.

Equipment and people
- Weighing scales
- Tape measure
- Thin flat object, such as a metal ruler

Interpreting results
Normative data on p.208 onwards.

Units: kg/m^2

Standard test method

First the participant is weighed:

- The participant removes their shoes and any heavy clothes such as coats.
- The participant stands still in the correct position on the scales. The tester takes the reading.

Next the participant's height is measured:

- The participant stands with their back flat against a wall. The tester places a flat object on top of the head so it is completely level. They make a small mark where the object touches the wall. The tester then measures the height of the mark from the floor.

BMI is then calculated as follows:

$$BMI = \frac{body\ weight\ (kg)}{height\ (m) \times height\ (m)}$$

The result is a number that can be anywhere between 12 and 60. A BMI of between 19 and 24 is considered to be a healthy weight.

For example, if Amol is 70kg and 1.8m tall then his BMI is as follows:

$$BMI = \frac{70}{1.8 \times 1.8}$$

$$BMI = \frac{70}{3.24}$$

$$BMI = 21.6$$

You will see from the normative data that this a healthy weight.

Reliability
Very reliable if measurements are accurate.

Practicality
✓ Cheap and easy to run the test

Validity
BMI is considered to be a reasonable indicator of the amount of body fat. However, BMI does not give a true picture of body composition for everyone – such as pregnant women, older people and muscular athletes. BMI may give misleading results for other individuals too. For a more accurate idea of body composition, other tests should be used.

Bioelectrical Impedance Analysis (BIA)

This test uses small electric currents running through the body to estimate the amount of body fat.

Equipment and people
- BIA machine

Interpreting results
Normative data on p.208 onwards.
Units: % body fat

Standard test method

In this test, a harmless electric current is run through the body. The total current that flows through the body depends on the amount of fat mass compared to fat-free mass. This is because the current flows less easily through fat than muscle.

To make an estimate of body composition, the participant's age, gender, weight, height and fitness must also be known.

- There are certain things the participant should or should not do in the hours before the test. They should:
    * drink plenty of water, as dehydration will overestimate body fat
    * avoid eating a large meal
    * avoid exercise.

- Before the test, the participant should be asked if they followed the eating, drinking and exercise guidelines above.

- The participant should stand with legs and arms apart. The participant should not be touching any other surfaces apart from the floor.

- Electrodes from the BIA machine may be placed on the participant, or they simply stand on metal footpads in bare feet. It depends on the machine's instructions.

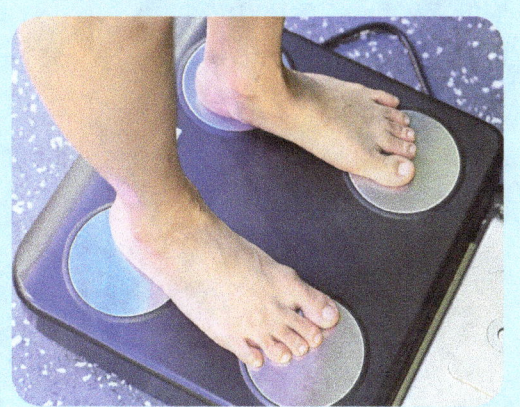

- Many machines also ask for the additional data about age, weight, height etc.

- The tester turns on the machine and it gives a percentage of fat mass and fat-free mass.

Reliability
Results are greatly affected by water in the body due to drinking, eating and exercise. This can make it hard to get reliable results.

Body temperature also affects readings

Practicality
✓ Easy to run the test

✗ Needs specialist equipment

✗ Only one person can be tested at a time

Validity
BIA machines measure electrical current. They then use this with normative data to estimate body composition for different ages, genders, weights and heights. This approach is generally considered a valid way to estimate body composition. However as results are affected by drinking, food and exercise, it is likely that results are not always completely accurate.

BIA results may be less valid for people with a high percentage of body fat.

Waist to hip ratio

This test compares waist and hip measurements.

Equipment and people
- A tape measure

Interpreting results
Normative data on p.208 onwards.

Units: measurements are in cm or inches but the WHR is a number without units

Standard test method
- The waist circumference is measured where it is smallest – normally near the belly button.
- The hip circumference is measured around the widest part of the hips.
- The waist-to-hip ratio (WHR) is calculated as:

$$WHR = waist\ (cm)\ /\ hips\ (cm)$$

WHR is seen as an indicator of health risks. The World Health Organization says that a WHR of 0.90 or higher (for men) and 0.85 or higher (for women) is a health risk.

Example: If Jonny's waist is measured as 86 cm and his hips are 96 cm then:

WHR = 86 / 96

= 0.8958

= 0.90 (rounded to two decimal places)

Reliability
This is a very reliable test if measurements are taken carefully.

Practicality
✓ Very cheap and easy to run
✓ Quick
✗ Can only test one person at a time

Validity
WHR is not a valid way to give an accurate percentage of fat and fat-free mass. So it is not valid to assess body composition for specific sports.

However, WHR can be used to track changes in fat and fat-free mass for an individual over time.

WHR is a valid indicator of general health and risk from various diseases and conditions.

Activity

Crispin competes in triathlons. He wants to test his aerobic endurance.

1. a) Name one aerobic endurance test that Crispin could complete.

Crispin's result from the Harvard Step Test is: **73**

The normative data for the test is:

Score	Rating
96+	Excellent
83-96	Good
68-82	Average
54-67	Below average
less than 54	Poor

b) State Crispin's rating for the Harvard Step Test.

Crispin struggles with the swimming part of the triathlon. He thinks he needs to focus on swimming training.

b) Name an aerobic endurance test that can be adapted for swimming.

c) Explain why it is important for Crispin to use this test.

Crispin joins a triathlon club. The club has a qualified coach.

d) i) State **one** other component of fitness that is important for the running part of the triathlon.

ii) Describe why this component of fitness is important for Crispin.

iii) Identify a fitness test that the coach can use for this component of fitness.

2. Identify each of the following fitness tests:

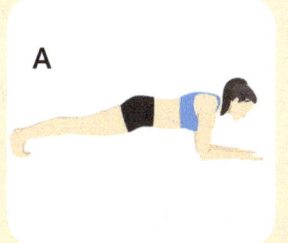

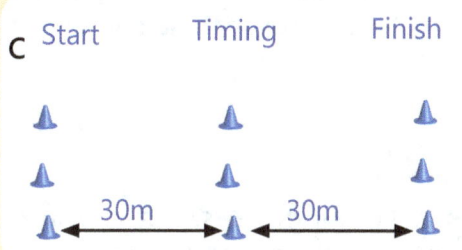

Jakub is a male gymnast who specialises in the rings. He wishes to understand more about his body composition.

3. Assess which body composition test Jakub should use by considering the reliability and validity of each method.

Lydia is a 200m sprinter working on her starts.

4. a) Describe the differences between the 30m Sprint Test and the 30m Flying Sprint Test.

b) Evaluate which test would be most suitable for Lydia.

B3 Fitness tests – agility

Illinois agility run test

This test measures how quickly someone can change direction whilst running forwards.

Equipment and people
- Flat running surface – it should not be slippy or wet
- Cones
- Stopwatch or timer
- Whistle

Interpreting results
Normative data on p.208 onwards.

Units: seconds

Standard test method
- The tester lays out the cones as shown in the diagram. There should be a 3.3m gap between the four cones in the middle section.
- The participant warms up.
- The participant lies face-down on the floor behind the Start cone.
- At the whistle the participant is timed as they run around the cones in the route shown in the diagram.
- Their time to reach the End cone is recorded.
- Participants should ideally have three attempts, recording only their best time. They should be given several minutes of recovery time between tests.

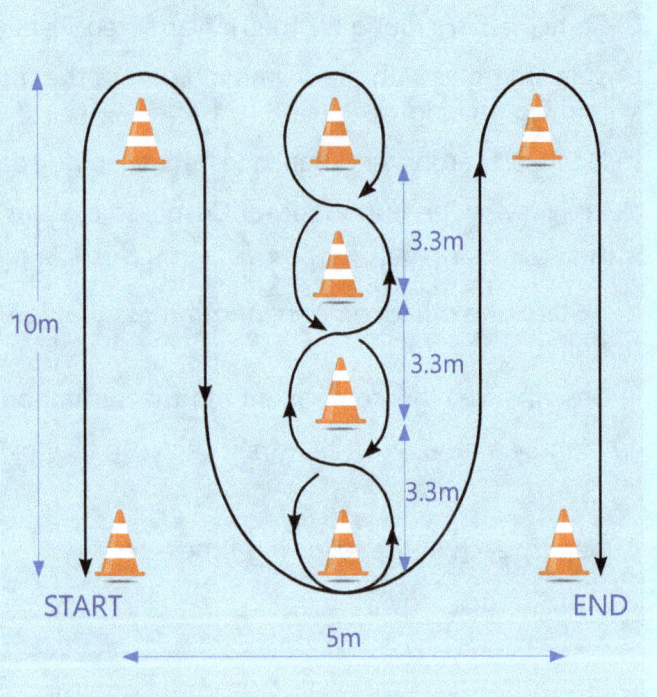

Reliability
Type of running shoes and running surface can affect the results.

Practicality
✓ Cheap and easy to run the test – not much equipment needed

✗ Only one participant can be tested at a time

Validity
The test is a valid predictor of agility whilst running forward.

Valid for sports that require changes of direction whilst running, such as hockey, rugby and netball.

As there are four sets of 10m sprints, a good sprinter with average agility can still get a good score. Other agility tests can provide an even better test of agility.

T test

This test measures how quickly people can move in different directions.

Equipment and people
- Flat running surface – it should not be slippy or wet
- Cones
- Stopwatch or timer
- Whistle

Interpreting results
Normative data are on p.208 onwards.

Units: seconds

Note that this test was created in the USA and is based on 10 yards, which is 9.14 metres. Most normative data is based on the 10 yards version.

Standard test method

- The tester lays out the cones as shown in the diagram.
- The participant warms up.
- The participant stands at cone A.
- At the whistle the timer is started and the participant sprints to cone B. They touch the base of cone B with their right hand.
- They then sidestep left until they reach cone C. They touch the base of cone C with their left hand.
- They then sidestep right until they reach cone D. They touch the base of cone D with their right hand.
- They then sidestep left until they reach cone B again. They touch the base of cone B with their left hand.
- Finally, they run backwards from cone B to cone A. The timer is stopped when they reach cone A.
- Participants should ideally have three attempts, recording only their best time. They should be given several minutes of recovery time between tests.

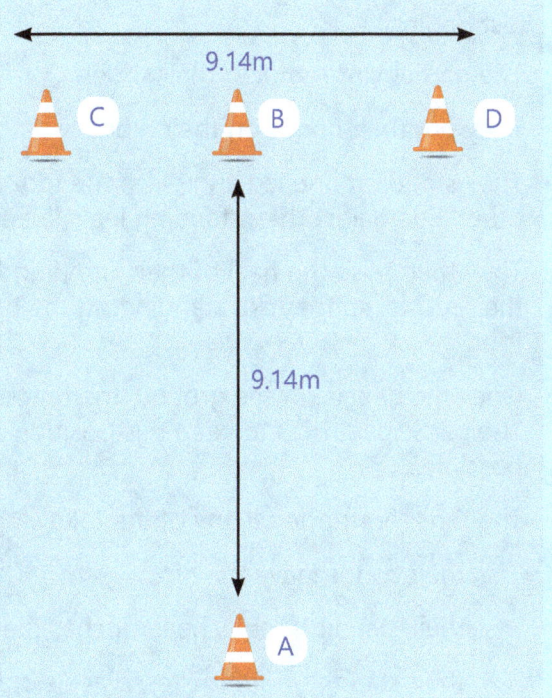

Participants should face forwards at all times during the test. The feet should not cross over each other during the sidesteps.

This test can be measured as 10 metres by 10 metres instead. But this affects any comparison of results with normative data.

Reliability
Type of running shoes and running surface can affect the results.

Different results for the 10 yard and 10 metre versions.

Practicality
✓ Cheap and easy to run the test – not much equipment needed

✗ Only one participant can be tested at a time

Validity
The test is a valid predictor of agility in all directions. It is valid for sports that require movement in all directions, such as tennis, volleyball and badminton.

Care should be taken when checking results with normative data. Much of the published data is for the 10 yard (9.14 metres) version of the test.

B3 Fitness tests – balance

Stork stand test

This test measures static balance.

Equipment and people
- Stopwatch or timer

Interpreting results
Normative data on p.208 onwards.

Units: seconds

Standard test method

The participant can be given a minute or two to practice the position described below before the test begins.

- The participant removes their shoes.
- They put their hands on their hips.
- They stand on one leg and place the foot of the other leg against their standing leg's knee.
- They then raise the heel of their standing foot off the ground, so they are standing on the ball of the foot.
- Once the heel is off the ground, the timer is started. The participant tries to keep this position as long as possible.
- The timer is stopped if any of the following happen:
    * their hands leave the hips
    * their standing foot's heel touches the floor
    * their standing foot moves, swivels or loses contact with the ground
    * their other foot is not touching the knee.
- The aim is to remain standing in position for as long as possible. The participant can be given three attempts, and the longest time recorded.
- The test can be repeated for the other leg.

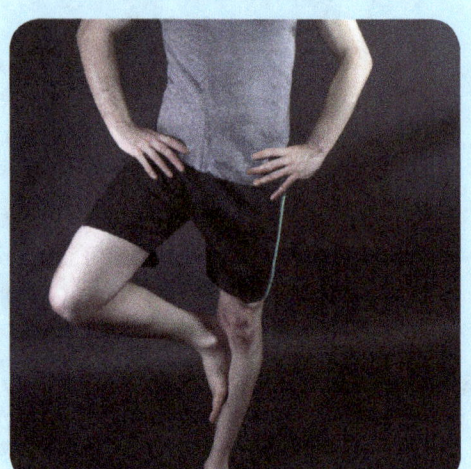

Reliability
This a reliable test when using the same leg.

Scores should record which leg was used.

Practicality
 Cheap and easy to run the test – only a timer is needed

 Only one participant can be tested at a time

Validity
This is a valid test for static balance.

It is valid for sports and activities such as gymnastics and yoga.

Y balance test

This test measures lower body balance in three directions.

Equipment and people
- Y-balance test equipment

Interpreting results
Normative data on p.208 onwards.

Units: cm

Standard test method
- Participants should warm up and then remove their shoes.
- The participant stands on the centre platform on one supporting foot. The longest toe is placed just behind the line.
- The non-supporting foot is placed behind the supporting foot.
- Participants put their hands on their hips.
- While standing on one leg, the participant uses their non-supporting foot to push the moveable platform in front of them as far as they can. They must then return the non-supporting foot to the central platform. The heel of the supporting foot is allowed to leave the platform.
- The tester notes down the distance the moving platform was pushed. (Most Y-balance equipment has the distances marked on poles.)
- This procedure is repeated for the other leg, and other moveable platforms.
- The whole test can be repeated and the best results in each direction taken as the score.

The standard order of the test is:
- right leg to front platform (A)
- left leg to front platform
- right leg to right platform (B)
- left leg to right platform
- right leg to left platform (C)
- left leg to left platform

Note that the participant may not:
- put their non-supporting foot down on top of the moving platforms
- kick the moving platforms
- put their foot down anywhere other than the central platform.

The results depend on the length of each participant's legs and body. However, to compare different people, we can calculate how far they can reach in each direction compared to their non-supporting leg:

Relative score % = 100 × (measured reach / length of leg)

Reliability
This is an indoor test.
The surface should not be slippy.

Practicality
✓ Easy to run the test
✗ Expensive – specialist equipment needed
✗ Only one participant can be tested at a time

Validity
The test is a valid predictor of balance in three different directions.

Valid for sports that require movement in all directions, such as tennis, volleyball and badminton.

B3 Fitness tests – coordination

Alternate-hand wall-toss test

This test measures hand–eye coordination.

Equipment and people
- Tennis ball
- Smooth vertical wall
- Masking tape
- Tape measure

Interpreting results
Normative data on p.208 onwards.

Units: number of catches

Standard test method
- The participant warms up whilst a line of masking tape is placed on the floor 2 metres from the wall.
- The participant is asked to throw the tennis ball underarm against the wall and catch it with the other hand. They then use this hand to throw the ball underarm back against the wall, and catch it with the original hand.
- The participant is timed for 30 seconds as they throw the ball from one hand to the other.
- The tester counts the number of catches they make in 30 seconds.
- The test can be repeated three times and the average number of catches calculated.

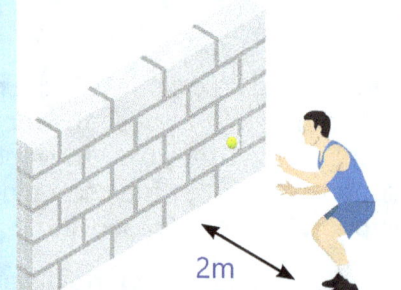

Reliability
Wind conditions can affect this test outdoors.

Results are also affected by how good the throws are. Adding a target to the wall to aim at will help with reliability.

Practicality
✓ Cheap and easy to run the test – does not need much equipment

✗ Only one participant can be tested at a time

Validity
This is a valid test for hand–eye coordination. It is highly valid for sports which include catching, such as softball, cricket and baseball.

It is not valid for other types of coordination, such as foot–eye coordination in football.

Stick flip coordination test

This test measures hand–eye coordination. It also measures the control of fine movements in the hands and wrists.

Equipment and people
- Three sticks, around 40–60cm long
- Masking tape (optional)

Interpreting results
Normative data on p.208 onwards.

Units: points

Standard test method
- To more easily track movements, wrap tape around one end of one stick.
- The participant holds two sticks in either hand.
- The tester places the stick with tape on top of the two sticks.
- There are two parts to the test: the half-flip, followed by the full-flip.

For the half-flip test:
- The participant tries to flip the stick over, so that it rotates through one half-turn. The taped end will point the other way for each flip.
- A successful half-flip scores 1 point.
- The participant has five attempts at a half-flip, so the maximum possible score is 5 points.

For the full-flip test:
- The participant tries to flip the stick over, so that it rotates through one full turn. This means the taped end will point the same way after each flip.
- A successful full-flip scores 2 points.
- The participant has five attempts at a full-flip, so the maximum possible score is 10 points.

The maximum possible score from the full test is 15 points. The test can be repeated to find an average score.

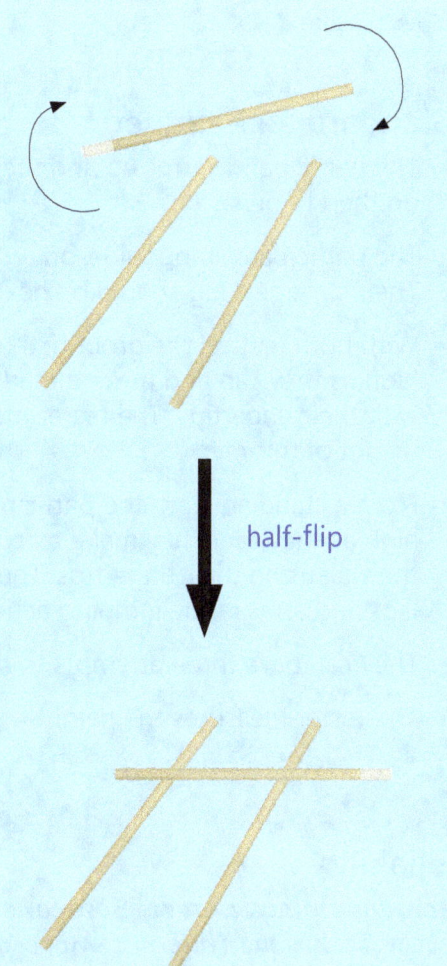

half-flip

Reliability
Wind conditions will affect results – test should be indoors.

The length of the sticks affects results.

Practicality
✓ Cheap and easy to run the test

✗ Whilst cheap, sticks are not standard equipment – they might not be in the department cupboard!

✗ Only one participant can be tested at a time

Validity
This test is only valid for a very specific type of hand–eye coordination.

It does not recreate actions in any particular sport, so it is not a valid predictor of performance in any sport.

B3 Fitness tests – power

Vertical jump test

This test measures lower body power.

Equipment and people
- Smooth vertical wall
- Chalk
- Tape measure
- Step ladder

Interpreting results
Normative data on p.208 onwards.

Units: cm

Standard test method
- The participant warms up and then places chalk on their fingers.
- The participant stands side-on against the wall. Their strongest leg should be next to the wall.
- With both feet on the ground, they reach up as high as they can and make a mark on the wall with their fingertips. The tester measures the height of this mark.
- From a standing start, the participant jumps as high as they can. They make a second mark on the wall using their fingertips. They can use their legs and arms in the jumping action.
- They can have three attempts to record the highest jump.
- The tester measures the height of the mark made by the highest jump.

Reliability
Technique plays a part. Someone with better technique (but not more power) can achieve better results.

Practicality
✓ Cheap and easy to run the test – does not need much equipment

✓ Small groups can perform the jumps at the same time

✗ Each measurement can only be done one at a time

Validity
This is a valid test of lower body power.

It is highly valid for sports which include vertical jumping, such as high jump, basketball and volleyball, cricket and baseball.

It is slightly less valid for sports which include horizontal jumping, such as long jump and triple jump.

Standing long jump test

This test is another measure of lower body power. It is also known as the standing broad jump test.

Equipment and people
- Tape measure
- Non-slip surface
- Chalk or masking tape

Interpreting results
Normative data on p.208 onwards.

Units: cm

Standard test method
- The participant warms up.
- The tester creates a start line on the floor, with chalk or tape.
- The participant stands with their feet just behind the line.
- The participant bends their knees and jumps with both feet. They can use their arms to help propel them forwards.
- They should try to land with both feet and not fall over.
- The tester measures the distance from the edge of the start line to the nearest contact the participant made with the ground. If they land on their feet this will be the back of their heel.
- The participant can have three attempts, with a few minutes' rest in-between. Their best attempt is used as their score.

Reliability
Wind conditions will affect results. Ideally the test should be arranged so any wind blows across the participant, rather than behind or in front of them. Ideally the test should be indoors.

Using a sandpit to land in will mean people with better technique will record longer distances. Avoid using sandpits.

Practicality
✓ Cheap and easy to run the test – very little equipment needed.

✗ Only one participant can be tested at a time.

Validity
This is a valid test of lower body power.

It is highly valid for sports which include horizontal jumping, such as long jump and triple jump.

It is slightly less valid for sports which include vertical jumping, such as high jump, basketball and volleyball.

Margaria Kalamen power test

This test is used to measure power in the lower body.

Equipment and people
- 12 equally-spaced stairs
- Weighing scales
- Tape measure or ruler
- Masking tape or chalk
- Stopwatch or timer

Interpreting results
Normative data on p.208 onwards.

Units: kg, metres and seconds

Standard test method

The test is based around running up stairs. The aim is to reach the 9th steps as quickly as possible.

- The participant warms up.
- The tester measures 6 metres away from the bottom step and marks out a start line.
- The tester weighs the participant in kilograms.
- The tester measures the height from the 3rd step to the 9th step. If the steps are the same height then one step height can be measured and multiplied by 6.
- The participant runs from the start line and up the stairs, standing on only the 3rd, 6th and 9th steps.
- The tester starts the timer when the participant's foot first touches the 3rd step. They stop the timer when their foot touches the 9th step.
- The participant can repeat the test three times and the fastest time taken as their score.

The participant's power can be calculated as follows:

$$\text{Power} = \frac{9.8 \times \text{weight (kg)} \times \text{height of steps (metres)}}{\text{time (seconds)}}$$

For example, Dani has a mass of 50kg and takes 0.60 seconds to climb stairs of height 1.05m. Her power is:

$$\text{Power} = \frac{9.8 \times 50 \times 1.05}{0.60}$$

$$= 514.5 / 0.60$$

$$= 857.5 \text{ Watts}$$

Reliability
Participants need to give their maximum effort.

Manual timing can introduce small errors.

Practicality
✓ Cheap and easy to run – not much equipment or space...

✗ ...but does require stairs

✗ Only one participant can be tested at a time.

Validity
Valid as a measure of the overall power to climb the stairs.

Valid for sports where lower body power is important – such as basketball, volleyball and sprinting.

B3 Fitness tests – reaction time

Ruler drop test
This test measures reaction time.

Equipment and people
- Ruler

Interpreting results
Normative data on p.208 onwards. **Units**: cm

An online test is available at:

https://cps-check.com/reaction-test

Standard test method
The aim of the test is to catch the ruler as soon as possible after it has been released.

- The participant extends their dominant forearm horizontally and holds out their thumb and index finger in an open grasp.
- The tester holds the bottom of the ruler between the participant's thumb and index finger. The 'zero' line of the ruler should line up with the top of the thumb or index finger. (Note: whether it is the thumb or index finger depends on which hand is being used and where the markings are on the ruler.)
- Without any warning, the tester lets go of the ruler.
- The participant catches the ruler between their thumb and index finger as soon as possible.
- The tester notes the position of the top of the thumb or index finger on the ruler. This measurement is how far the ruler dropped before being caught.
- The test can be repeated a number of times and an average distance calculated.

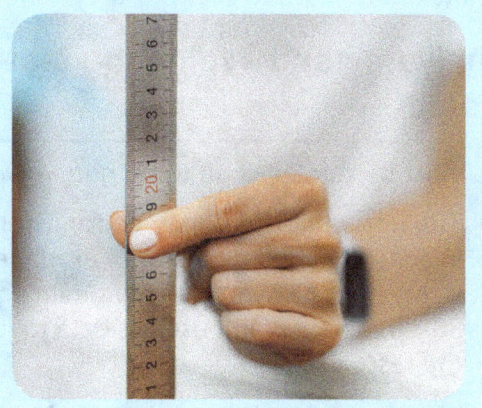

Reliability
Initial distance between thumb and index finger affects result.

Ruler must be dropped, not pushed downwards.

Practicality
✓ Very easy and cheap to run – only a ruler is needed

✗ Can only test one participant at a time

Validity
The test is a valid measure of reaction time. It is particularly valid as a measure of the reaction time of hands and fingers.

Particularly valid for sports where the hands react to a stimulus – such as racket sports, goalkeeping in football, and motor racing.

Online reaction time tests
There are many reaction time tests online or as apps. They measure the time to respond to something on-screen. These tests are very reliable. They are also practical as long as you can access a computer or smartphone.

They are also a valid measure of reaction time but slightly favour people who use computers or smartphones a lot.

B4 Interpretation of fitness test results

After completing a test, you need to be able to understand the results.

Normative data

Researchers conduct tests with different groups of people and publish the results. This is called **normative data**.

The tests are run very carefully to make sure the results are reliable.

The number of participants in the research is called the **sample size**. If the sample size is big enough then we can get an idea of what is a good, poor and average result.

Normative data allows us to compare the results of our tests, to see how they compare.

Analysing and evaluating test results

We must be careful when using normative data:

- **The normative data may be for a very specific age and gender.** For example, if the normative data is for women aged 30–40 then we can't use the data to judge the results of a 15-year-old boy.
- **The normative data might have been collected from athletes.** The people in the study might be athletes who are training all the time. Their scores in many tests will be much better than the average non-athlete and should not be used to compare with non-athletes.
- **Some normative data is based on a small sample size.** Care should be taken when assuming a small sample represents the general population.

To interpret our test results we need to:

- compare our result with the normative data, and check that we are using the right units (for instance, using metres not inches)
- find the correct age and gender category
- see which category our result falls into, such as Very Good, Good, Average and so on.

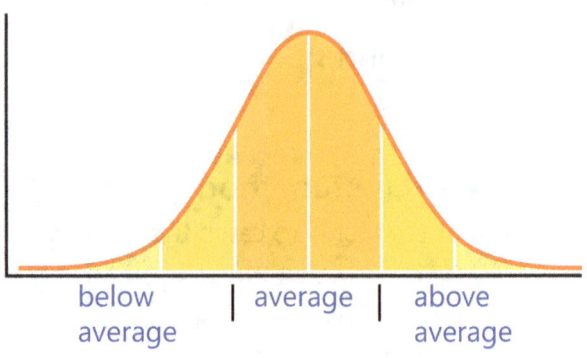

below average | average | above average

Recommendations

Interpreting test results gives us an idea of how the participant's fitness compares with others. This allows us to recommend training that will benefit them in their given sport or activity.

Example

For example, a striker in football receives the following:

- a good rating in the 30 metre sprint test
- an excellent rating in the 30 metre flying sprint test results
- an average rating in the Margaria-Kalamen power test.

The first two results suggest that the striker has a fast top speed but her acceleration could be improved.

The third result suggests that working on increasing lower-body power would help with her acceleration.

So, a training plan that focused on power in the acceleration phase would really benefit her game.

Activity

1. Describe how to run the Margaria-Kalamen power test.

2. Mike is a basketball player. He has been following a training plan. He took three different tests at two different times during the plan.

He had the following results:

Test	Rating in week 1	Rating in week 6
A: Vertical jump test	Good	Good
B: Y-balance test	Good	Excellent
C: Horizontal jump test	Average	Excellent

a) Assess how effective Mike's training has been.

b) Describe the differences in validity between Test A and Test C.

3. Match each of the following tests with the sport it is most valid for.

A: Alternate-hand wall-toss   1 Badminton

B: Stork stand test   2 Gymnastics

C: T test   3 Cricket

4. Orla plays table tennis. She is asked to test her agility levels.

a) Describe the differences between the Illinois Agility Run Test and the T-Test.

b) Explain which test would be most suitable for Orla.

c) In the T-test Orla's result is 'Average' when compared to normative data.

Identify where her result sits on the graph of normative data.

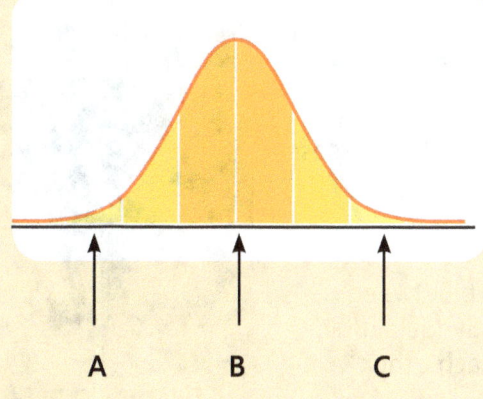

A   B   C

C1 Requirements for fitness training methods

Each fitness training session should

- start with a warm-up
- end with a cool-down
- link to specific components of fitness
- apply the FITT principle, and additional principles of training
- use the right level of intensity.

> **Intro**
>
> Discuss what you think might happen if you don't perform a warm-up before exercise

See section A2 in this component for more on FITT and principles of training

Warm-up

Every training session must begin with a warm-up. A warm-up is important because it:

- reduces the chance of injury
- prepares the body for the activity.

The warm-up should last for 10-20 minutes.

There are three parts to a warm-up. They should take place in order as follows.

Pulse-raiser

In this part of the warm-up:

- the heart rate gently increases
- breathing rate gently increases
- blood flow gently increases, so more oxygen reaches muscles
- muscle and body temperature increase.

Typical pulse-raiser activities include jogging, and sport-specific activities such as:

- side steps in football
- 'bum kicks' for runners
- jumping and hopping for netball and basketball.

Pulse-raisers should slowly but steadily increase in intensity.

Mobility

Joints are where two bones meet. Between the two bones is **synovial fluid**. Synovial fluid allows the bones to glide over each other.

Mobility exercises focus on gently moving and rotating joints. This encourages production of synovial fluid allowing joints to move freely and fully.

Mobility exercises include:

- arm rotations
- foot rotations
- shoulder dips
- high steps.

Stretching

The range of motion at a joint also depends on the muscles that are attached to it. Muscles need to be gently stretched so each joint has a full range of motion.

Stretching exercises focus on the main muscles that will be used in the training activity.

There are two types of stretching:

- **static stretching** – where the stretch is held in place for a short amount of time
- **dynamic stretching** – where the stretch is part of a body movement.

Cool-down

Every training session must end with a cool-down. A cool-down is important because it:

- Helps to remove lactic acid from the body
- Restores muscles to their pre-exercise length

The cool-down should last for 5-10 minutes.

There are two parts to a cool-down. They should take place in order as follows.

Lowering the pulse

When you exercise, waste products such as **lactic acid** build up in the muscles.

The muscles rely on the flow of blood to clear these waste products.

If you just stop moving after exercising then breathing rate, heart rate and blood flow decrease rapidly. Less blood reaches the muscles, which means lactic acid is not removed very quickly.

In a cool-down you gently decrease exercise intensity. This reduces breathing rate, heart rate and blood flow more gradually. This means that blood continues to reach the muscles and clear away lactic acid.

Pulse-lowering activities gradually decrease in intensity. For example, after a training run, a cool-down could include:

- reducing the pace to very easy...
- ...then reducing the pace to a gently jog...
- ...then reducing the pace to a brisk walk...
- ...before reducing to a slow walk, and then finally stopping.

Stretching

Muscles work hard by constantly contracting and relaxing during an exercise session. This means that muscles can be shorter at the end of the session than at the start.

Stretching helps to restore muscles to their original length. This restores flexibility and helps prevent injury.

Activity

Jimmy always warms-up before playing rugby but never cools down

1. a) Describe how a cool-down helps recovery after exercise.

b) Identify which of these joints is most important for Jimmy to mobilise in his warm-up:

A: Neck B: Hip C: Toe

c) Give an example of a pulse-raiser that would be suitable for Jimmy.

C2 Fitness training methods for physical components of fitness

Aerobic endurance

The cardiorespiratory system provides oxygen to our muscles. To improve aerobic endurance we need to train the system to deliver more oxygen to muscles.

Good aerobic endurance allows us to run, cycle or row at a faster pace for longer.

Aerobic endurance training is important for any sport or activity that lasts for longer than 30 minutes.

There are four training methods to improve aerobic endurance.

Intro
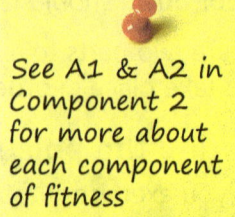
Which components of fitness are important for your favourite sport

See A1 & A2 in Component 2 for more about each component of fitness

Continuous training

Continuous training means exercising at a low to moderate intensity (60–80% HR Max) for more than 30 minutes.

This training gives the cardiorespiratory system a workout.

Training at too high an intensity engages the anaerobic system. This does not help with aerobic endurance.

It is a common mistake to think that training is not working unless it feels very hard. This is wrong! Elite long-distance runners spend most of their training running at a comfortable pace.

Intervals

Intervals are short, high-intensity workouts followed by short rests. They should be around 85% HR Max.

Whilst intervals are short, they should be long enough to engage the aerobic system – at least 60 seconds long.

Whilst aerobic intervals also engage the anaerobic system, they work the aerobic system very hard. This is okay because each workout is short. The rest allows the body to recover before the next workout.

Circuit training

Circuit training consists of a number of different aerobic exercise stations.

Each station has a different aerobic exercise, designed to raise the heart rate. They could

include exercises such as skipping, jumping, step-ups and burpees.

Participants complete the exercise at each station in a circuit, with a short rest period between stations. They can repeat the circuit several times.

Fartlek

Fartlek is a Swedish word. It means 'speed play'.

It is a form of continuous exercise where the intensity varies dramatically.

It is made up of longer stretches of low to moderate intensity but with short bursts of intense exercise at certain points.

Fartlek was originally developed for runners. There is no formal structure to a Fartlek session. But it does need to:

- mix up exercise intensity
- make sure there is enough low intensity work to recover.

Flexibility

Flexibility is important to make sure joints can move through their full range of motion.

There are three methods to improve flexibility.

Static active stretching

This is when someone stretches their own muscle.

They apply a force and hold the stretch for 10–20 seconds.

- **static** – no movement whilst stretching.
- **active** – use own body to apply a force to stretch the muscle.

Static passive stretching

This is when someone uses another person or object to hold the stretch.

Once in position they hold the stretch for 10–20 seconds.

- **static** – no movement whilst stretching.
- **passive** – use another object to apply a force to stretch the muscle.

PNF stretching

PNF stands for **Proprioceptive Neuromuscular Facilitation**.

This type of stretching requires a partner or object.

1. Participant stretches their muscle as far as it will go, and holds it for a short time.
2. Partner holds the body part in position. Participant pushes hard against the partner using the muscle for a short time.
3. The participant then relaxes the muscle.
4. The partner then moves the body part and stretches the muscle slightly beyond it's original position.
5. Steps 2-4 is repeated one or two times.

PNF stretching is good when muscles are very tight, or after injury.

However, if performed incorrectly PNF stretching can cause significant injury. Only people with a lot of experience should attempt it.

Activity

1. Identify **one** type of aerobic endurance training that uses the **variation** principle of training.

Toni is a high jumper who trains alone.

2. a) Explain why stretching is important for Toni.

b) Identify the most appropriate type of stretching for Toni.

Muscular endurance

Muscular endurance is how long a muscle can keep working at a low to medium intensity. The key to muscular endurance training is:

Low weight
High repetitions

Free weights and fixed resistance machines

Free weights include dumbbells, barbells and kettlebells.

Fixed resistance machines are special pieces of equipment. They are most often found in gyms.

The weight on these machines can be increased or decreased as required.

Typical session:
five sets of
- *12 reps*
- *50–60% 1RM*

Circuit training

Circuit training for muscular endurance is made up of a number of exercise stations. A short amount of time is spent at each station, with a short rest in between stations.

Each station focuses on different muscle groups. The stations might use:

- free weights (low loads)
- the body's own weight – for instance, in a tricep dip.

In circuit training the same rules apply – low weights and high reps.

Muscular strength

Muscular strength is the largest force that a group of muscles can generate. The key to muscular strength training is:

High weight
Low repetitions

Free weights and fixed resistance machines

Free weights and fixed resistance machines can also be used for muscular strength training.

Typical session:
three sets of
✓ 6 reps
✓ 85-90% 1RM

Activity

Emma and Ryan are working out at the gym.

1. Emma completes 5 reps of a 40kg bench press. Ryan completes 10 reps of a 40kg bench press.

Copy and complete the table below:

Name	High or low reps?	Endurance or strength training?
Emma	....	....
Ryan	....	....

2. Felicity would like to increase her lower body muscular endurance for running. However her local gym is a national chain and too expensive for her.

a) Name the type of provision offered by her local gym.

b) Describe how Felicity could still increase her lower body muscular endurance.

Speed

Special training is needed to increase top speed and to run fast for longer.

Acceleration sprints

The runner begins from either a standing start or a gentle jog.

They gradually increase speed, moving through to strides. Strides should be around 70-80% of maximum pace.

Speed continues to increase up to a maximum sprint.

After keeping top speed for a short period, the runner slows down and recovers.

Resistance drills

Resistance drills make running harder than normal. They help to build strength and power, and develop good running form.

- Hill runs – even gentle hills can make running harder.
- Parachutes and sleds – these both attach to the back and slow the runner down. They provide a constant resistance against the runner.

- Bungee ropes – these elastic ropes attach to the back. They pull the runner back with a larger and larger force until the runner stops. Bungee ropes are good for working on acceleration.
- Resistance bands – there are a number of drills using resistance bands wrapped around the legs. This extra resistance develops strength in muscles that are used to run fast. Drills include 'monster walk' and 'banded side-steps'.

Intervals

Intervals are a series of short and fast runs with rest periods in between.

- Speed training intervals should be shorter but more intense than endurance training intervals. Intensity means close to maximum sprinting speed.
- The rest periods for speed training intervals should be longer and more frequent than endurance training intervals.

Activity

Helen is training for a 10km run. She is an experienced runner but has recently recovered from a thigh strain. She does not have access to any special equipment.

Her training plan for week 1 is as follows:

Day	Session
Monday	Rest day
Tuesday	Speed intervals
Wednesday	Muscular endurance
Thursday	Easy 3km run
Friday	Rest day
Saturday	Resistance drills
Sunday	Long, easy 12km run

1. a) Describe one type of training that would be suitable for Wednesday's session.

b) Name two days on which Helen trains for speed.

c) i) Name the training zone suitable for Sunday's long run.

ii) Describe how Helen could use the Borg rating in Sunday's run.

iii) Name a fitness test that could be used to track improvements in Helen's aerobic endurance.

d) Explain which resistance drill you would recommend for Helen.

Helen rarely warms up properly for any of her training.

e) Explain why a warm-up is important.

f) Assess the most appropriate type of stretching for Helen.

g) State the other two components of a warm-up.

h) Describe the effect that a cool-down has on lactic acid.

2. a) Describe the changes you would expect in this plan by week 4.

b) State the fitness training principle that is the reason for these changes.

C3 Fitness training methods for skill-related components of fitness

Agility

Agility training is important in any sport where the athlete needs to change direction quickly

Speed Agility and Quickness (SAQ) training

> **Intro**
> Which components of skill-related fitness are important for your favourite sport?

This type of training combines sprinting and changes of direction.

This training often uses cones, ladders, poles, hoops and hurdles.

SAQ training drills are specific to each sport. Examples include:

- dodging around cones for rugby
- side stepping over mini hurdles for football
- sprinting, side-stepping and shuffling around poles in tennis
- manoeuvring around cones in wheelchair basketball.

Coordination

Coordination is being able to move and position two or more parts of the body at the same time.

Coordination training is sport-specific. This is because the demands of each sport are different. For instance, the coordination to execute a tennis serve is very different to the coordination in a long jump, or a somersault in parkour.

Some examples of coordination drills include:

- Ball-catching practice in rugby.
- In tennis, bouncing a ball on alternate racket heads as many times in a row as possible.

Reaction time

Reaction time is how quickly someone can respond to an external event.

There are some special machines to train reaction time, using lights or buttons. These machines also test hand–eye coordination.

However, most reaction time training is sport-specific. Examples include:

- Point-blank goalkeeper training in football. A partner stands very close and throws the ball in different directions for the goalkeeper to save.
- Using tennis-ball machines to practise returning high-speed serves.

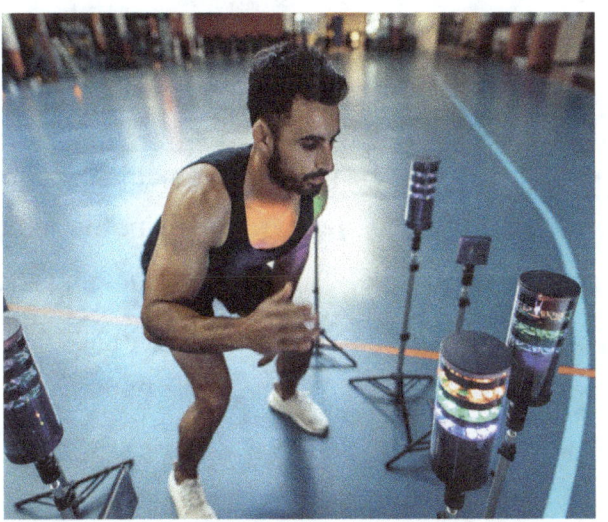

Power

Power combines strength and speed. It means applying large forces in short, sharp bursts.

Plyometrics

Plyometrics is the name for a group of exercises where the muscles generate:

> maximum force for a short amount of time.

There are different forms of plyometrics. For example:

- incline and clapping press-ups
- jumping and barrier hopping
- lunging
- bounding

In each exercise, the performer uses the maximum force possible. This causes the muscles to lengthen and then shorten very quickly.

Applying the force in shorter amounts of time increases the power.

For example, when jumping onto a box:

- the performer should try and jump as high as possible
- the action of straightening the leg when launching off the ground should be as quick as possible.

Balance

Balance is the ability to stay upright.

- **Static balance** means staying upright whilst standing still.
- **Dynamic balance** means staying upright whilst moving.

Static balance

To train static balance, the participant stays in the same position for a period of time. Some positions include:

- standing completely upright with feet together
- standing completely upright with one foot in front of the other
- standing on the heel of both or either foot
- standing on only one foot
- using balance boards.

The base of support can be reduced, as in the last three examples, to increase the challenge as balance improves.

Static balance training can also be sport-specific. For instance, some positions in gymnastics are unique.

Dynamic balance

Dynamic balance training adds movement:

- standing on one leg whilst moving the other leg in different positions
- repeat as above but then jumping onto the other foot and repeat
- tandem walking (placing each foot directly in front of and touching the other foot)
- backwards tandem walking
- using a balance board whilst moving some parts of the body.

These kind of exercises can be made more difficult by performing them in reverse or with the eyes closed.

Good balance also requires good coordination and muscle strength in the legs and core.

Dynamic balance training can also be sport-specific. For example:

- one-legged head-tennis in football
- diagonal bounding for badminton, whilst holding the racket
- 'ice-skater' side-to-side bounding for tennis.

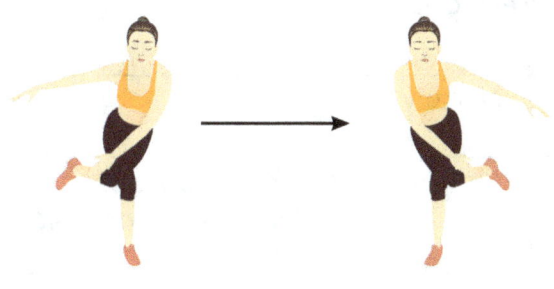

C4 Advantages and disadvantages of each fitness training method

Aerobic endurance

Continuous training

	Advantage	Disadvantage
Number of people that can take part	✓ Lots at same time	
Cost of equipment	✓ No equipment	
Ease of set up	✓ Easy to set up and can be done alone	
Access to venue	✓ No special venue needed for running or cycling	
Risk of injury	✓ Low risk as below maximum effort	✗ Injury can occur if distance is stepped up too quickly
Specificity to fitness	✓ Effective for increasing aerobic endurance	

Effectiveness of training for specific sports:

✓ Building good aerobic endurance is important in any sport where activity lasts for more than 30 seconds. However continuous training is more suited to longer events, e.g. (800m+ track), cycling, swimming and team sports where plenty of distance is covered in a match e.g. football, rugby, hockey

Intervals

	Advantage	Disadvantage
Number of people that can take part	✓ Lots at same time	
Cost of equipment	✓ Cheap - stopwatch	
Ease of set up	✓ Easy to set up ✓ Can be done alone	
Access to venue		✗ Ideally need a track or GPS watch, so distance can be measured
Risk of injury		✗ Max effort means greater injury risk
Specificity to fitness	✓ Effective for increasing aerobic endurance	✗ Intervals need to be long enough to target aerobic rather than anaerobic system

Effectiveness of training for specific sports:

✓ Aerobic intervals are suitable for any sport where aerobic endurance is important. But they are particularly useful for sports with short bursts of running and rests in between e.g. tennis, football, netball

Circuit training

	Advantage	Disadvantage
Number of people that can take part		✗ Limited by the number of stations
Cost of equipment	✓ Can be done with little or no equipment...	✗ ...but some equipment may be necessary
Ease of set up	✓ Can be done alone	✗ If using equipment, takes time to set up
Access to venue	✓ Not necessary to have a special venue...	✗ ...but some equipment may only be available in a gym
Risk of injury	✓ Depends but short routines help reduce risk	
Specificity to fitness	✓ Can be effective...	✗ ...but the correct length and type of exercises have to be chosen

Effectiveness of training for specific sports:

✓ Very effective as the exercise stations can be tailored to the sport in question

✓ Variety of different exercises helps prevent boredom

Fartlek

	Advantage	Disadvantage
Number of people that can take part	✓ Lots at same time	
Cost of equipment	✓ No equipment	
Ease of set up	✓ Easy to set up and can be done alone	
Access to venue	✓ No special venue needed for running or cycling	
Risk of injury	✓ Low risk as maximal efforts are short	
Specificity to fitness	✓ Effective for increasing aerobic endurance...	✗ ...but a lot the training is done by 'feel' which means it can be hard to measure progressive overload

Effectiveness of training for specific sports:

✓ Fartlek training is suitable for any sport where aerobic endurance is important. But it is particularly useful for sports with intermittent aerobic effort and sprinting e.g. road cycling stage races, handball, ice hockey

✓ Variety helps prevent boredom

Flexibility

Static active stretching

	Advantage	Disadvantage
Number of people that can take part	✓ Lots at same time	
Cost of equipment	✓ No equipment	
Ease of set up	✓ Easy to set up ✓ Done alone	
Access to venue	✓ No special venue needed	
Risk of injury	✓ Fairly low risk if proper technique is followed	
Specificity to fitness	✓ Effective for a range of muscles	✗ Not all muscles can be targeted with active stretching

Effectiveness of training for specific sports:

✓ Different static active stretches can be used for specific sports

✗ Other stretches are needed for some sports e.g. passive hamstring stretch for rugby

Static passive stretching

	Advantage	Disadvantage
Number of people that can take part	✓ Lots at same time	
Cost of equipment	✓ Common equipment can be used	
Ease of set up	✓ Easy to set up	✗ Partner may be needed
Access to venue	✓ No special venue needed	
Risk of injury		✗ Slightly higher risk as technique is more important
Specificity to fitness	✓ Effective for a range of muscles that can't be targeted with active stretching	

Effectiveness of training for specific sports:

✓ Different passive stretches can be used for specific sports

PNF stretching

	Advantage	Disadvantage
Number of people that can take part		✗ One at a time with experienced partner
Cost of equipment	✓ Inexpensive equipment such as table or mat	
Ease of set up		✗ Experienced partner is required
Access to venue	✓ No special venue needed...	✗ ...but generally needs to be done indoors
Risk of injury		✗ Muscle is being pushed beyond its normal limit. High risk of injury if partner has no experience of PNF
Specificity to fitness	✓ Effective for a range of muscles that can't be targeted with active stretching	

Effectiveness of training for specific sports:

✓ Different PNF stretches can be used for specific sports

✗ More suitable for post-injury recovery or very tight muscles

Muscular endurance and strength

Free weights

	Advantage	Disadvantage
Number of people that can take part		✗ Limited by number of weights available
Cost of equipment	✓ Relatively cheap	✗ Specialist equipment
Ease of set up	✓ Easy to set up...	✗ ...but do need to follow correct techniques ✗ Strength – spotter needed
Access to venue	✓ No special venue needed – weights available at home	
Risk of injury	✓ Endurance – less chance of injury as weight not close to maximum	✗ Strength – risk of injury as weight is near maximum. ✗ Both – injury risk if not using right technique
Specificity to fitness	✓ Can be used for lots of different muscle groups	

Effectiveness of training for specific sports:

✓ Free weights are very flexible and can be adapted for the specific sport

Fixed resistance machines

	Advantage	Disadvantage
Number of people that can take part		✗ Only one per machine
Cost of equipment		✗ Very expensive
Ease of set up	✓ Easy to set up – good for the less experienced and can be done alone	
Access to venue		✗ Only normally available at gyms
Risk of injury	✓ Less risk of injury – machine helps stop body moving in wrong direction	
Specificity to fitness	✓ Multiple machines can be used for lots of different muscle groups	✗ Each machine can only target one muscle group

Effectiveness of training for specific sports:

✓ With access to enough different machines, endurance and strength for specific sports can be targeted

✗ Some actions in some sports may be harder to replicate using fixed resistance machines

Circuit training

If using free weights within the stations then the advantages and disadvantages are as discussed for them before. The following lists the advantages and disadvantages of using body weight resistance exercises:

	Advantage	Disadvantage
Number of people that can take part	✓ Lots at same time	
Cost of equipment	✓ No equipment necessary	
Ease of set up	✓ Easy to set up and can be done alone	
Access to venue	✓ No venue needed	
Risk of injury	✓ Less risk of injury using body weight	
Specificity to fitness	✓ Can be used for lots of different muscle groups ✓ Better for endurance	✗ Not as easy to overload some muscles using body weight alone – harder to optimise for muscular strength

Effectiveness of training for specific sports:

✓ Endurance and strength for specific sports can be targeted by different exercises

✗ Endurance and strength in muscle groups for some sports can be easier to target with free weights or machines

Speed

Acceleration sprints

	Advantage	Disadvantage
Number of people that can take part	✓ Lots at same time	
Cost of equipment	✓ No equipment	
Ease of set up	✓ Easy to set up and can be done alone	
Access to venue		✗ Need a high-quality flat surface with plenty of space. Other surfaces e.g. grass playing field carry greater risk of injury at high speed
Risk of injury		✗ Max effort means greater injury risk
Specificity to fitness	✓ Effective for increasing speed and acceleration	

Effectiveness of training for specific sports:

✓ Good for any sport where reaching top speed quickly is important e.g. 100m sprint, long jump, rugby (backs), football (outfield)

Interval training

	Advantage	Disadvantage
Number of people that can take part	✓ Lots at same time	
Cost of equipment	✓ No equipment	
Ease of set up	✓ Easy to set up and can be done alone	
Access to venue		✗ Ideally need a track or GPS watch, so distance can be measured
Risk of injury		✗ Max effort means greater injury risk
Specificity to fitness	✓ Very effective at increasing speed	✗ Intervals need to be short enough to target anaerobic system

Effectiveness of training for specific sports:

✓ Good for any sport where sprinting speed is important, e.g. 200m track, triple jump, lacrosse

Resistance drills

	Advantage	Disadvantage
Number of people that can take part	✓ Hill runs – lots at same time	✗ Depends on equipment for parachutes, sleds etc.
Cost of equipment	✓ Hills – no equipment	✗ Other equipment is specialist and not cheap
Ease of set up	✓ Hills – easy	✗ Other drills take a bit of time to set up with the right equipment
Access to venue		✗ Need to find hills ✗ Specialist venues for other equipment
Risk of injury		✗ Additional resistance means greater injury risk
Specificity to fitness	✓ Effective for increasing muscle strength and power	✗ More effective for top speed when used alongside other speed drills

Effectiveness of training for specific sports:

✓ Effective for sports where power, strength and speed are important, such as rugby, basketball and track sprinting

✓ Variety of different methods reduces boredom

Agility

Speed, Agility and Quickness (SAQ)

	Advantage	Disadvantage
Number of people that can take part	✓ Lots at same time	
Cost of equipment	✓ Equipment is fairly cheap	
Ease of set up		✗ Takes a bit of time to set up the equipment drills
Access to venue	✓ Can be set up anywhere	
Risk of injury		✗ Quick changes of direction puts greater strain on muscles and joints
Specificity to fitness	✓ Effective for agility training	

Effectiveness of training for specific sports:

✓ Effective for sports with a change of direction, such as basketball, badminton, rugby

✓ Training is made specific for each sport

Coordination

	Advantage	Disadvantage
Number of people that can take part	✓ Lots at same time...	✗ ...unless numbers are limited by access to equipment
Cost of equipment	✓ If equipment is used it is normally cheap	
Ease of set up	✓ Depends but many drills are quite simple to set up	
Access to venue	✓ Can be done anywhere	
Risk of injury	✓ Little risk for simple drills...	✗ ...but some sport-specific drills carry greater risk e.g. some movements in gymnastics
Specificity to fitness	✓ Effective for the specific type of coordination in the drill	

Effectiveness of training for specific sports:

✓ Coordination training is most effective when it is sport-specific

Reaction time

	Advantage	Disadvantage
Number of people that can take part	✓ Lots at same time...	✗ ...unless numbers are limited by access to equipment
Cost of equipment	✓ If equipment is used it is normally cheap...	✗ ...but some equipment can be more expensive
Ease of set up	✓ Depends but many drills are quite simple to set up	
Access to venue	✓ Depends on the drill	
Risk of injury	✓ Little risk for simple drills...	✗ ...but some sport-specific drills may carry greater risk e.g. sprinter reacting to starter gun
Specificity to fitness	✓ Effective for the specific reaction time in the drill	

Effectiveness of training for specific sports:

✓ Reaction time training is most effective when it is sport-specific

Power

	Advantage	Disadvantage
Number of people that can take part	✓ Lots at same time...	✗ ...unless numbers are limited by access to equipment
Cost of equipment	✓ If equipment is used it is fairly cheap	
Ease of set up	✓ Easy to set up ✓ Can be done alone	
Access to venue	✓ Can be set up anywhere	
Risk of injury		✗ Using maximum force in shortest time puts a larger strain on muscles and joints
Specificity to fitness	✓ Effective to develop power	✗ Only effective for the specific muscle groups in the drill

Effectiveness of training for specific sports:

✓ Drills can be made sport-specific

Balance

	Advantage	Disadvantage
Number of people that can take part	✓ Lots at same time...	✗ ...unless numbers are limited by access to equipment
Cost of equipment	✓ Equipment not often necessary but if used it is fairly cheap	
Ease of set up	✓ Easy to set up ✓ Can be done alone...	✗ ...but should only be done alone if balance is already quite good
Access to venue	✓ Can be set up anywhere	
Risk of injury	✓ For people already with good balance, the risk is quite small	✗ Falling over can cause serious injuries, so there is a much greater risk for people with poor balance, older people and those carrying injuries
Specificity to fitness	✓ Depends on the drill but generally effective	✗ Only effective for the specific type of balance in the drill

Effectiveness of training for specific sports:

✓ Drills should be made sport-specific

C5 Provision for taking part in fitness training methods

Fitness training can be offered by different types of providers. There are advantages and disadvantages of each type.

> See section A1 in Component 1 for more public, private and voluntary provision

Public provision

Public sector provision is funded by the government. They may still charge people to use their services but the charges are normally less than the private sector.

These organisations do not make a profit.

Examples:

- school sports
- local authority swimming pool,
- outdoor gym in a park

Advantages	Disadvantages
✓ Common sports and activities covered ✓ Provides access for a wide range of people	✗ Unlikely to cover minority sports or activities
✓ Equipment is cheaper or free to borrow or use	✗ Equipment more likely to be older and more basic
✓ Cheaper than private sector ✓ Some provision or facilities are free e.g. outdoor gyms ✓ Discounts for certain groups, e.g. pensioners	✗ Fewer or no additional services such as childcare, cafe

Private provision

Private sector provision is through private companies.

They are funded by the owners and charging for their services e.g. membership fees.

They have to make a profit.

Examples:

- The Gym Group
- Fitness First.

Advantages	Disadvantages
✓ Wide range of sports and activities	✗ Minority sports are not covered ✗ Provision depends on where you live
✓ Lots of the latest expensive equipment	✗ There may be extra cost to hire or use speciality equipment
✓ May provide subsidies for certain groups e.g. students	✗ Can be expensive
✓ Offers a wide range of classes, activities and treatments	✗ Expense stops a wide range of people taking part
✓ Access to additional services, such as childcare, café	

Voluntary provision

Voluntary provision is when people give up their time for free. Most grass-roots sports clubs are run by volunteers who are passionate about sport.

They are funded through donations, fundraising, and membership fees.

These organisations do not make a profit.

Examples:

- Parkrun
- local amateur cricket, football and tennis club.

Advantages	Disadvantages
✓ Lots of different provision including minority sports ✓ Fills gaps left by public and private sector	✗ Covers only one sport or activity
✓ Can focus on gaps in provision so may have equipment not available elsewhere...	✗ ...but facilities and equipment can be limited
✓ Provision can be free or very low cost	✗ Unlikely to have additional services
✓ Provides access to a huge range of sports and activities ✓ Also provides access to a wide range of people	

Activity

John is a 100m sprinter. He trains with a local amateur athletics club.

1. a) Describe the principle of plyometric training.

b) Give **one** example of a plyometric leg training exercise.

c) State how plyometric training would benefit John.

d) Give **one** disadvantage of plyometric training.

e) What kind of sports provision does John use?

f) Stage **one** advantage and **one** disadvantage of this provision.

Darius plays tennis for fun with friends twice a week.

2. a) i) Describe the **two** different types of balance. ii) Give an example of a training exercise for each kind of balance.

b) State which kind of balance training would best suit Darius.

Darius also likes to go to yoga classes.

c) Explain how effective this kind of training is for yoga.

Darius plays tennis and goes to yoga at a private gym.

d) Give **two** reasons why Darius might choose this type of provision.

e) State one other skill-related component of fitness that is relevant to tennis.

Ella joined a local judo club. She takes a number of different fitness tests. Her results are as follows.

Test	Rating
Reaction time	Below average
Agility	Good
Flexibility – Sit and Reach Test	Excellent
Muscular endurance	Average

3. a) Describe how to carry out the Sit and Reach Test.

To maintain her flexibility, Ella uses passive stretching.

b) State **one** reason why Ella uses passive stretching instead of active stretching.

Ella trains her muscular endurance using fixed resistance machines.

c) State **two** advantages to using fixed resistance machines instead of free weights.

d) Explain why Ella does not plan to include resistance drills in her training.

The judo club meets in a church hall and is run by volunteers.

e) Explain why the local private sports club does not run judo classes.

C6 The effects of long-term fitness training on the body systems

Aerobic endurance training

Aerobic endurance training causes the cardiovascular and respiratory systems to adapt.

These adaptations are what makes training work.

> **Intro**
>
> Discuss which kind of training you find the most and least enjoyable.

Cardiovascular system

The cardiovascular system is made up of the heart, blood vessels and blood.

Cardiac hypertrophy

The heart is a muscle. When a muscle is trained regularly it gets bigger. This is known as hypertrophy.

Cardiac hypertrophy means that the heart increases in size – the walls of the heart become thicker and stronger. As a result, it can pump more blood around the body in each heartbeat.

Decreased resting heart rate

- Cardiac hypertrophy means the heart can pump more blood around the body in one heartbeat. This means more oxygen is sent around the body in each heartbeat.
- This is in turn means the heart can pump the same amount of oxygen in one minute with fewer heartbeats.

Cardiac hypertrophy means the heart does not have to work as hard to supply oxygen. This means you can continue to exercise at a moderate intensity for longer.

A decrease in resting heart rate is a sign that aerobic endurance is increasing.

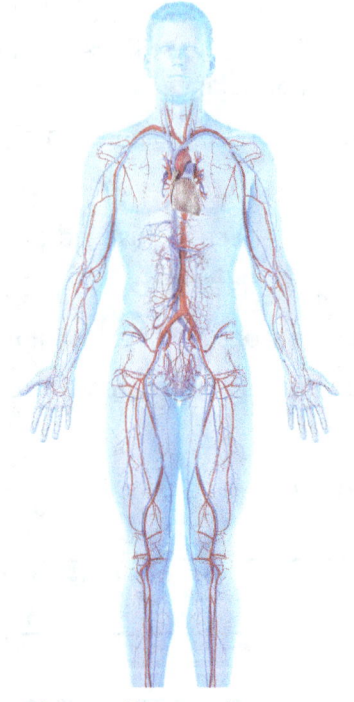

The cardiovascular system

> **cardiovascular system** the heart, blood vessels and blood
>
> **respiratory system** the organs used for breathing

Respiratory system

The respiratory system is made up of the lungs, the tubes that link the mouth to the lungs, the alveoli, and the respiratory muscles.

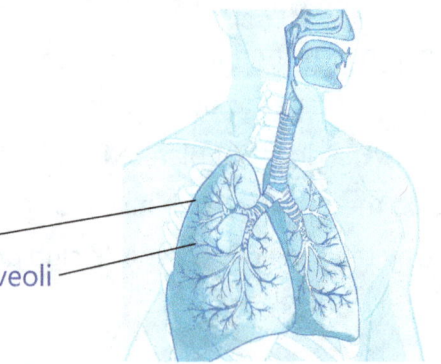

Increased strength of respiratory muscles

There are two sets of muscles that allow us to breathe:

- the diaphragm
- the intercostal muscles between the ribs.

Aerobic endurance training works these muscles. Like any muscle, they get stronger with training.

Stronger respiratory muscles means breathing becomes more efficient, allowing:

- more oxygen to pass into the blood in each breath
- more waste products to be removed from the blood in each breath.

Capillarisation around the alveoli

The alveoli are tiny grape-like structures deep in the lung. There are millions of alveoli in a human lung. All the oxygen you breathe in ends up in the alveoli.

The alveoli are where oxygen enters the bloodstream. They are also where carbon dioxide is removed from the bloodstream, to be breathed out.

- The alveoli are surrounded by tiny blood vessels called capillaries.

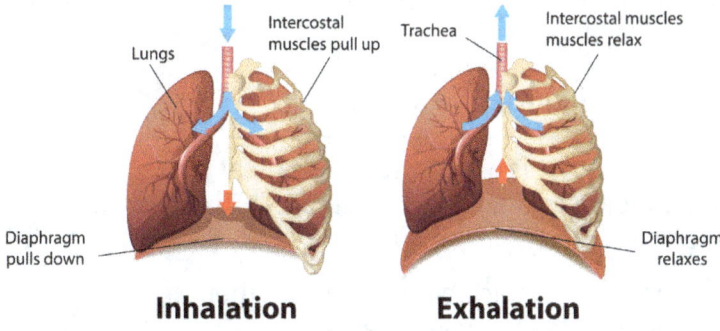

The respiratory muscles. Inhalation means breathing in, and exhalation means breathing out.

> **capillarisation** an increase in number of capillaries

Both capillarisation and stronger breathing muscles mean more oxygen can be sent to the muscles used for exercise.

The more oxygen a muscle receives, the longer it can continue working at a moderate intensity. This increases aerobic endurance.

- Aerobic endurance training encourages more capillaries to form around the alveoli.
- This means even more oxygen can enter the bloodstream in each breath.

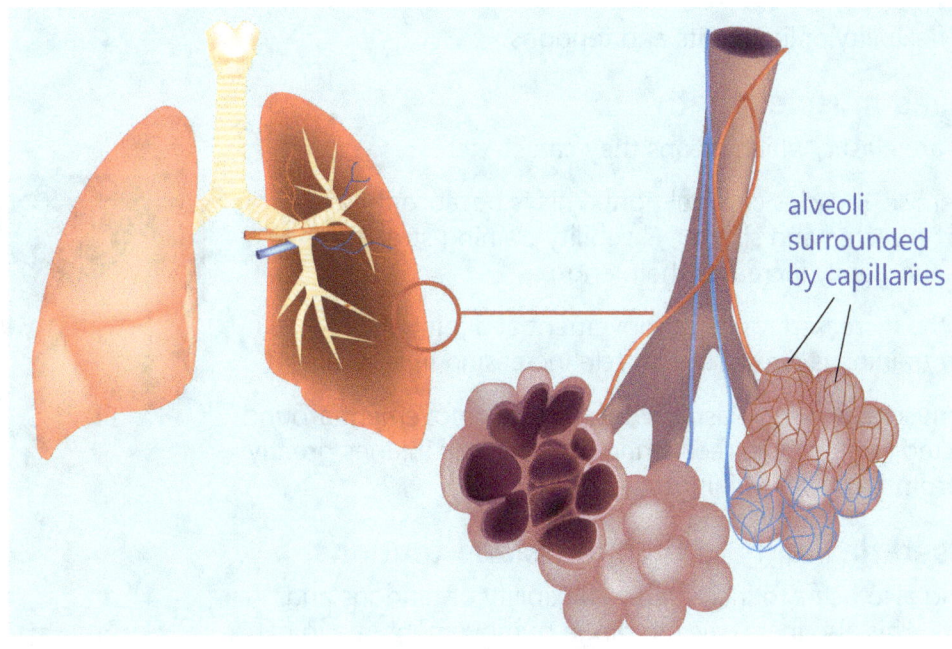

alveoli surrounded by capillaries

Flexibility training

To understand how flexibility training works, we need to look at the structure of joints.

Synovial joints

A synovial joint is where two bones meet but are not directly attached to each other. This allows movement in the joint.

- Ligaments attach bones to each other. Ligaments keep joints stable.
- Tendons attach muscles to bones. Tendons allow muscles to move bones.
- Muscles move joints by pulling on tendons, which then pull on the bones.
- The ends of the bones are covered with cartilage and the space between them is filled with synovial fluid.

Range of movement at a joint

Different joints allow different types of movement. The range of movement at a joint depends on:

- The type of joint. For example, your knee joint is only meant to move in one direction.
- The health of the cartilage and synovial fluid, as these allow the bones to glide over each other.
- The length of the muscles.
- The flexibility of ligaments and tendons.

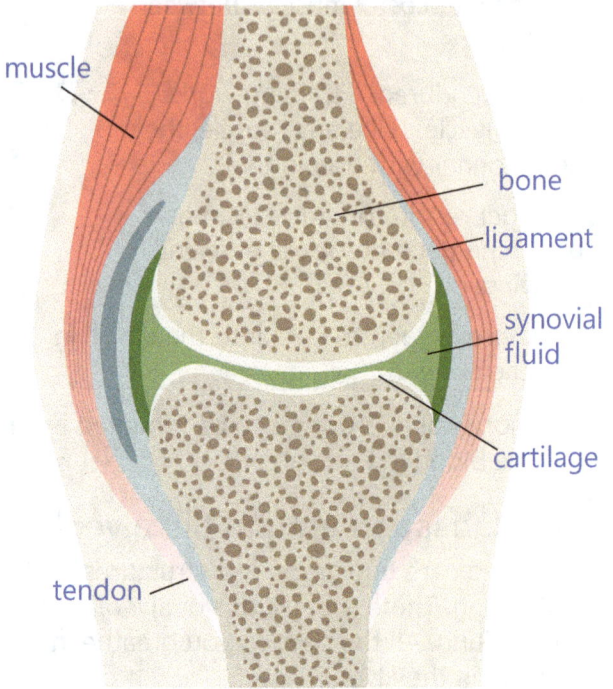

A synovial joint

Increased muscle length

Muscles are elastic, which means they can stretch.

After exercise, muscles can feel tight. This is because they are slightly contracted and shorter. Flexibility training stretches muscles and gently increases their length.

Most of the increased range of movement at a joint after flexibility training is due to the muscle increasing in length.

Injured muscles are less elastic, which reduces movement around the affected joint. People recovering from muscle injuries greatly benefit from flexibility training.

Increased flexibility of ligaments and tendons

Stretching also helps to increase the flexibility of tendons and ligaments. This also increases the range of movement at a joint.

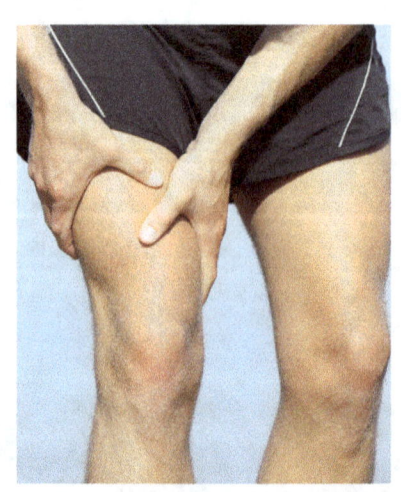

Muscular endurance training

Muscular endurance training causes adaptations to the muscular system.

Capillarisation around muscles

Small blood vessels called capillaries deliver blood to muscles.

- Capillary walls are so thin that they allow oxygen from blood to travel across the wall and into the muscle.
- Capillaries also remove waste products from the muscles.
- Muscular endurance training encourages more capillaries to surround the muscles that are trained.
- This allows more oxygen to reach each muscle. Getting more oxygen to the muscle means it can continue working at moderate intensity for longer.
- This also allows more waste products to be removed from the muscles. This is important because the sensation of muscle fatigue is due to the build up of waste products in muscles.

Structure of a muscle

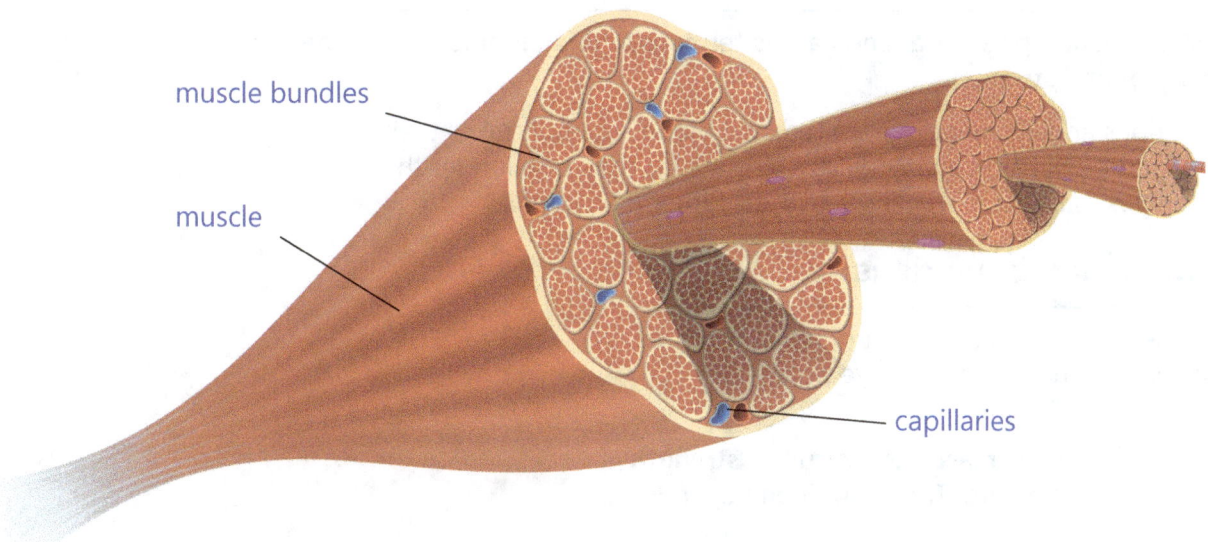

Increased muscle tone

Muscle tone is resistance to movement even when the muscle is relaxed. This is because muscles are still slightly contracted, even when relaxed.

- Good muscle tone is important for good posture.
- Muscles with good tone store more energy when relaxed. Some of this energy can be used during movement, such as walking or running. This means that a well-toned muscle does not have to work as hard as a poorly-toned muscle..
- Muscles with good tone can react quicker to external forces – for instance, a misplaced foot when walking). This protects joints and helps prevent injury.

Muscular endurance training increases muscle tone.

Muscular strength and power training

Muscular strength and power training causes adaptations to the muscular and skeletal systems.

> hypertrophy increase in size

Muscle hypertrophy

A large percentage of a muscle's mass is protein.

Muscle proteins are constantly broken down and removed. But new muscle proteins are also constantly created.

Under normal conditions, protein breakdown happens at the same rate as protein creation, and muscles stay the same size.

However, strength training promotes a higher rate of protein creation. This has the effect of building muscle mass.

Strength training leads to greater protein creation because the muscles adapt to the stress caused by overload.

Increased tendon and ligament strength

Strength and power training causes tendons and ligaments to become thicker and stronger.

Tendons and ligaments have a reduced blood supply. It takes them longer to heal after an injury. This also means they take longer than muscles to adapt to training – months rather than weeks.

Increased bone density

Bone density is the amount of mineral content of bones. These minerals give bones their strength.

Bone density increases as a result of strength and power training. The adaptation depends on:

- **How much force** is placed on the bone: muscular strength training (using heavier weights) encourages greater bone density.
- **How rapidly the force is applied**: power training, such as plyometrics, encourages greater bone density.

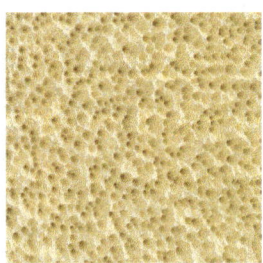

The left-hand image is a cross section of a healthy bone,. The right-hand image is a bone with severely low bone density.

Bones are constantly renewed. Old, worn-out cells are destroyed and new cells take their place. When you reach the age of 35, bone density begins to decrease. This leads to weak bones in later life.

Strength and power training is recommended for people over 35, in order to maintain bone density.

Speed training

Speed training causes adaptations to the muscular system.

> **lactic acid** a waste product created by muscles as they work

Increased tolerance to lactic acid

- Exercising at a high level of intensity engages the anaerobic energy system. This energy system produces **lactic acid**.
- The body can clear a certain amount of lactic acid. But if intense exercise continues, lactic acid builds up in the bloodstream.
- A build-up of lactic acid is associated with burning sensations in muscles, and feelings of intense discomfort, telling you to slow down or stop.
- Speed training consists of short but intense bouts of exercise in which lactic acid builds up. However, the rest periods between exercise allows the body to clear lactic acid again.
- Speed training adapts the body so that it becomes better at clearing lactic acid. It also becomes better at operating with higher levels of lactic acid present.

Activity

1. a) Explain what the term 'cardiac hypertrophy' means.

b) State what kind of training leads to cardiac hypertrophy.

2. Describe how capillarisation around muscles develops muscular endurance.

3. Explain why muscular strength training is particularly important for people over the age of 35.

4. a) Describe the difference between a tendon and a ligament.

b) State **two** things that happen to the body due to flexibility training.

Jing is a sprint track cyclist.

5. a) Identify which of the following is the most important for Jing:

A: Muscular strength **B**: Flexibility **C**: Speed

Jing also needs to improve her power.

b) i) State one power test that would be suitable for Jing. ii) Describe the validity of using this test for Jing.

c) State **one** reason why fitness testing is useful.

d) Give the name of **one** form that Jing should fill out before beginning the test.

Jack plays football. His position is on the left wing. He needs to improve his coordination and speed.

6. a) State **one** training method that would improve Jack's running speed.

ii) Describe the effect of speed training on Jack's body.

b) Assess the importance of muscular endurance and power for footballers.

D1 Personal information to aid training fitness programme design

Before designing fitness training programmes, you first need to understand what the performer wants to get out of the programme, and their level of fitness.

> **Intro**
>
> Write down your aims and objective for your BTEC Tech Award Sport.

Aims and objectives

Aims are what the performer want to achieve.

Objectives are how the performer will meet their aims.

> For example, Julie is an enthusiastic runner who took up running aged 36.
> - Her aim is to run a 26 minute 5k.
> - Her objective is to develop her aerobic endurance using continuous training and intervals, in order to meet her aim.

Lifestyle and activity

Two of the additional principles of training are:
- Individual differences – this means the training must be specific for the individual.
- Progressive overload – this means the training must not be too hard or too easy, and must increase in difficulty over time.

To apply these principles we need to know about the performer's:

Lifestyle
- diet
- smoking and alcohol
- sleep and stress.

Health
- physical activity
- work – is it physically active?
- how much exercise they do each week.

Medical history

We need to know if there are any medical reasons that might stop the performer from training, or change the kind of training they should do.

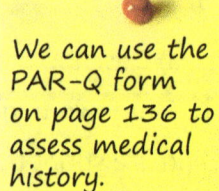

We can use the PAR-Q form on page 136 to assess medical history.

Attitude and personal motivation

We saw in Learning Outcome B that personal motivation has a big effect on the results of fitness tests.

The same is true of fitness training. If the performer is not motivated to give all their effort in each session, or regularly misses sessions, then the training will not work as planned.

- Fitness training has to mirror the performer's level of motivation and availability. For example, a training programme with sessions 5 days a week might not work for a parent with two small children – even though the parent might be very motivated, they simply can't commit that amount of time to training.

- There may be some types of training which the performer does not like, or gets easily bored of. Knowing this in advance helps you to develop appropriate training plans.

D2 Fitness programme design

Selecting appropriate training

To select an appropriate training method you need to think about the following:

- What are the performer's stated aims and objectives?
- What sports or activities are they training for?
- What are the important components of fitness for their chosen sports or activities?

    * Aerobic endurance
    * Flexibility
    * Muscular endurance
    * Muscular strength
    * Speed
    * Agility
    * Power
    * Balance
    * Coordination
    * Reaction time

- Which of these components do they need to a) improve, b) maintain?

For each component, list the possible training methods, as described in sections C2 and C3.

By doing all this, you will ensure the training is specific for the sport or activity in question.

Application of the principles of training using personal information

Once you have a list of possible training methods for relevant components, you need to apply the FITT principles and additional principles of training.

The FITT principles are:

Frequency, Intensity, Time, Type.

The additional principles are:

- progressive overload
- specificity
- individual differences
- adaptation
- reversibility
- variation
- rest and recovery.

To fully apply these principles you need to carefully consider the performer's personal information.

- First you must ensure the training will be safe for the performer. If they have ticked 'yes' to any question in the PAR-Q form then a medical professional should be consulted before going ahead with training.

- Secondly, you must take into account the performer's lifestyle and activity levels. For example, a light smoker and drinker, with an office job and no recent history of aerobic exercise would really struggle to start with a hard interval session of 8 × 400m running.

- You can use fitness testing for each component of fitness you have identified, to get a better idea of where the performer is weak or strong. Note that the performer might be very good at some components and weak in others.

- Their personal information, and any fitness test results, inform the frequency, intensity and time of the training sessions. This ensures you are considering individual differences.

You then need to examine the performer's motivation and attitudes, to further tweak the plan. For example:

- If a performer is very busy, and only available on Monday night, Tuesday morning and Friday afternoon, then either the Monday or Tuesday session must be very light, or focus on a completely different component of fitness.

- Alternatively, if the performer hates doing long runs at the same pace, then you might need to change the type of session e.g. increase the length of fartlek sessions but decrease interval session times to compensate.

- For the training plan to work, **there must be enough rest** in order that the body can adapt. And then the plan must increase in difficulty to ensure adaptation continues through progressive overload.

- **Consideration must also be given to reversibility**. For example, holidays might interrupt a longer-term training plan. In this case, some simpler self-guided sessions might be appropriate, to at least maintain performance until the normal sessions can resume.

- Finally – even the most well thought-out sessions don't always go according to plan! You can **tweak the plan as you go along** if you continue to monitor:
    * how the performer is doing
    * how they are feeling
    * and continue to apply the principles of training.

Activity

Alastair has joined a new gym. Before his first session he has been asked about his aims, objectives and lifestyle.

1. a) Describe the difference between an aim and an objective.

b) Explain why it is important to know about Alastair's lifestyle before designing a training plan.

c) State one other piece of information that the gym should know about Alastair.

d) State what a PAR-Q form is used for.

D3 Motivational techniques for fitness programming

Motivation is the drive that someone has to do or achieve something.

Types of motivation

There are two types of motivation:

Intrinsic motivation comes from within. It is an 'inner drive'. Examples include:

- enjoyment of the sport or activity
- a desire to maintain or improve fitness
- satisfaction in improving
- enjoyment of the challenge
- the feeling of achievement.

Extrinsic motivation comes from external factors. Examples include:

- beating someone else
- being the best
- winning a prize
- earning money
- acclaim from other people.

Intro

"Motivation is more important than natural ability"

Discuss this statement. Do you agree? Why?

Setting goals

Setting goals is a useful way to direct, maintain and increase motivation.

Goals should be **SMARTER**:

Specific – a specific goal is one in which you consider precisely who is going to do what. You can also consider why they are going to do it – for example, as part of the performer's overall aim.

Measurable – goals must be measured in some way. 'I want to cycle quicker' is not a measurable goal. 'I want to maintain an average speed of 20km/hour on the bike part of a sprint triathlon' is a measurable goal.

Achievable – the goal must be a level of performance that the performer could actually achieve – for example, running a 12 second 100m would be unachievable for many people, no matter how much training they did.

Realistic – the goal must be realistic – for example, it might be very achievable for a good 5k runner to complete a marathon in under 3 hours. But a 6 week training plan would be unrealistic, as they would need more time to build up to marathon distances

Recorded – the steps towards the goal should be captured in some way – for example, GPS watches record data which shows how the performer is moving towards their goal.

Exciting – for maximum motivation, the goals should be something the performer really wants to do, and which will result in exciting performances in their sport or activity.

Time-related – the goal must have a stated timeframe.

To really help with motivation, there should be a number of different goals.

Long-term goals have a timeframe measured in months or even years.

- They provide an overall direction for all the training.
- They ensure that the training will lead to specific achievements, and the effort will yield results.

Short-term goals have a timeframe measured in days or weeks, up to one month.

- They provide structure to long-term goals.
- They also allow the performer to focus on activities each week, and see improvements and achievements in the short term. This helps maintain and even increase motivation.
- Without short-term goals, training can feel aimless, which affects motivation.

Benefits of motivation

Motivation has a big impact on a performer.

Increased participation

Motivated performers will turn up to almost every session.

They will do so even if:

- tired
- the weather is not good
- other events in their life clash with sessions.

Maintain training and intensity

Motivated performers will not give up when things get harder.

They will maintain their intensity and try hard through all sessions – even those that they find difficult, painful or slightly boring.

Increased fitness and performance

Attending most sessions, and ensuring they get the most out of training by trying hard, means that motivated performers reap the benefits from training:

- They will show improvement in their selected components of fitness.
- And, because the training plan was carefully designed, they will show improvement in their chosen sport or activity.

Activity

Mimi is 25 and has recently started playing hockey for a local team. She used to play at school to a high standard. The hockey team play in a league and Mimi is feeling very motivated.

Mimi has set herself some goals using the SMARTER personal goals. She wants to score two goals by the time she has played three games.

1 a) Copy and complete the table:

i) State the name of each SMARTER goal

ii) Give an example of each using Mimi's goals.

Letter	Name of SMARTER goal	Example
M		
T		

iii) Mimi plays in defence. Discuss whether you think her goals are SMARTER.

Mimi's goals above are short-term.

2. a) Give a SMARTER long-term goal for Mimi.

b) Describe the benefits to Mimi of setting goals.

3. Evaluate the potential impact of intrinsic and extrinsic motivation on Mimi's performance in the hockey team that season.

Normative data tables

Multistage Fitness Test

Male

Age	very poor	poor	fair	average	good	very good	excellent
14-15	< 4.7	4.7-6.1	6.2-7.4	7.5-8.9	8.10-9.8	9.9-12.2	> 12.2
16-17	< 5.1	5.1-6.8	6.9-8.2	8.3-9.9	9.10-11.3	11.4-13.7	> 13.7
18-25	< 5.2	5.2-7.1	7.2-8.5	8.6-10.1	10.2-11.5	11.6-13.10	> 13.10
26-35	< 5.2	5.2-6.5	6.6-7.9	7.10-8.9	8.10-10.6	10.7-12.9	> 12.9
36-45	< 3.8	3.8-5.3	5.4-6.4	6.5-7.7	7.8-8.9	8.10-11.3	> 11.3
46-55	< 3.6	3.6-4.6	4.7-5.5	5.6-6.6	6.7-7.7	7.8-9.5	> 9.5

Female

Age	very poor	poor	fair	average	good	very good	excellent
14-15	< 3.3	3.3-5.2	5.3-6.4	6.5-7.5	7.6-8.7	8.8-10.7	> 10.7
16-17	< 4.2	4.2-5.6	5.7-7.1	7.2-8.4	8.5-9.7	9.8-11.10	> 11.10
18-25	< 4.5	4.5-5.7	5.8-7.2	7.3-8.6	8.7-10.1	10.2-12.7	> 12.7
26-35	< 3.8	3.8-5.2	5.3-6.5	6.6-7.7	7.8-9.4	9.5-11.5	> 11.5
36-45	< 2.7	2.7- 3.7	3.8- 5.3	5.4-6.2	6.3-7.4	7.5-9.5	> 9.5
46-55	< 2.5	2.5-3.5	3.6-4.4	4.5-5.3	5.4-6.2	6.3-8.1	> 8.1

Source: https://www.topendsports.com/testing/norms/beep.htm

Yo-Yo test

	male		female	
rating	metres	level	metres	level
elite	> 2400	> 20.1	> 1600	> 17.5
excellent	2000-2400	18.7-20.1	1320-1600	16.6-17.5
good	1520-1960	17.3-18.6	1000-1280	15.6-16.5
average	1040-1480	15.7-17.2	680-960	14.6-15.5
below average	520-1000	14.2-15.6	320-640	13.1-14.5
very poor	< 520	< 14.2	< 320	< 13.1

Source: https://www.topendsports.com/testing/norms/yo-yo.htm

Harvard Step Test

Score	Rating
96+	Excellent
83-96	Good
68-82	Average
54-67	Below average
less than 54	Poor

Source: https://www.topendsports.com/testing/tests/step-harvard.htm

12-minute Cooper test
Running

Age	Excellent	Above Average	Average	Below Average	Poor
Male 20-29	> 2800m	2400 - 2800m	2200 - 2399m	1600 - 2199m	< 1600m
Males 30-39	> 2700m	2300 - 2700m	1900 - 2299m	1500 - 1999m	< 1500m
Males 40-49	> 2500m	2100 - 2500m	1700 - 2099m	1400 - 1699m	< 1400m
Males 50+	> 2400m	2000 - 2400m	1600 - 1999m	1300 - 1599m	< 1300m
Females 20-29	> 2700m	2200 - 2700m	1800 - 2199m	1500 - 1799m	< 1500m
Females 30-39	> 2500m	2000 - 2500m	1700 - 1999m	1400 - 1699m	< 1400m
Females 40-49	> 2300m	1900 - 2300m	1500 - 1899m	1200 - 1499m	< 1200m
Females 50+	> 2200m	1700 - 2200m	1400 - 1699m	1100 - 1399m	< 1100m

Source: https://www.topendsports.com/testing/norms/cooper-12minute.htm

1-minute press-up test

Age	Excellent	Good	Average	Fair	Poor
Male 20 - 29	>54	45 - 54	35 - 44	20 - 34	<20
Male 30 - 39	>44	35 - 44	25 - 34	15 - 24	<15
Male 40 -49	>39	30 - 39	20 - 29	Dec-19	<12
Male 50 - 59	>34	25 - 34	15 - 24	Aug-14	<8
Male 60+	>29	20 - 29	Oct-19	05-Sep	<5
Female 20 - 29	>54	45 - 54	35 - 44	20 - 34	<20
Female 30 - 39	>44	35 - 44	25 - 34	15 - 24	<15
Female 40 -49	>39	30 - 39	20 - 29	Dec-19	<12
Female 50 - 59	>34	25 - 34	15 - 24	Aug-14	<8
Female 60+	>29	20 - 29	Oct-19	05-Sep	<5

MACKENZIE, B. (2001) Press Up Test [WWW] Available from: https://www.brianmac.co.uk/pressuptst.htm [Accessed 5/4/2023]

1-minute sit-up test

Men: Age	18-25	26-35	36-45	46-55	56-65	65+
Excellent	>49	>45	>41	>35	>31	>28
Good	44-49	40-45	35-41	29-35	25-31	22-28
Above average	39-43	35-39	30-34	25-28	21-24	19-21
Average	35-38	31-34	27-29	22-24	17-20	15-18
Below Average	31-34	29-30	23-26	18-21	13-16	11-14
Poor	<31	<29	<23	<18	<13	<11

Women: Age	18-25	26-35	36-45	46-55	56-65	65+
Excellent	>49	>45	>41	>35	>31	>28
Good	44-49	40-45	35-41	29-35	25-31	22-28
Above average	39-43	35-39	30-34	25-28	21-24	19-21
Average	35-38	31-34	27-29	22-24	17-20	15-18
Below Average	31-34	29-30	23-26	18-21	13-16	11-14
Poor	25-30	22-28	17-22	13-17	9-12	7-10

Source: https://www.topendsports.com/testing/tests/home-situp.htm

Timed plank test

Rating	Excellent	Very good	Above average	Average	Below average	Poor	Very poor
Time	> 6 minutes	4-6 minutes	2-4 minutes	1-2 minutes	30-60 s	15-30s	< 15s

Source: https://www.topendsports.com/testing/tests/plank.htm

Sit and reach test

Male: Age (years)	20 – 29	30 – 39	40 – 49	50 – 59	60 – 69
Excellent	≥ 29	≥ 27	≥ 24	≥ 24	≥ 22
Very Good	23 – 28	22 – 26	18 – 23	17 – 23	14 – 21
Good	19 – 22	17 – 21	13 – 17	13 – 16	9 – 13
Fair	14 – 18	12 – 16	7 – 12	5 – 12	4 – 8
Poor	≤ 13	≤ 11	≤ 6	≤ 4	≤ 3

Dingley, E (2021). Sit and Reach Test.

Available from: https://sportscienceinsider.com/sit-and-reach-test/ [Accessed 18/5/2023].

Female: Age (years)	20-29	30-39	40-49	50-59	60-69
Excellent	≥ 30	≥ 30	≥ 27	≥ 28	≥ 24
Very Good	26 – 29	25 – 29	23 – 26	22 – 27	20 – 23
Good	22 – 25	21 – 24	19 – 22	19 – 21	16 – 19
Fair	17 – 21	16 – 20	14 – 18	14 – 18	12 – 15
Poor	≤ 16	≤ 15	≤ 13	≤ 13	≤ 11

Shoulder flexibility test

Rating	Men	Women
Excellent	<17.8cm	<12.7cm
Good	17.8 - 29.2cm	12.7 - 24.8cm
Average	29.2 - 36.8cm	24.8 - 33.0cm
Fair	36.8 - 50.2cm	33.0 - 45.1cm
Poor	>50.2cm	>45.1cm

Adapted from: MACKENZIE, B. (2007) Static Flexibility Test - Shoulder [WWW] Available from: https://www.brianmac.co.uk/flextest4.htm [Accessed 13/5/2023]

30m sprint test

Gender	Excellent	Above Average	Average	Below Average	Poor
Male	<4	4.0 - 4.2	4.3 - 4.4	4.5 - 4.6	>4.6
Female	<4.5	4.5 - 4.6	4.7 - 4.8	4.9 - 5.0	>5.0

These data are for 16-19 year olds. MACKENZIE, B. (1999) Flying 30 metre Test [WWW] Available from: https://www.brianmac.co.uk/flying30.htm [Accessed 25/5/2023]

30m flying sprint test

Gender	Excellent	Above Average	Average	Below Average	Poor
Male	<2.6 secs	2.6 - 2.9 secs	2.9 - 3.1 secs	3.1 - 3.3 secs	>3.3 secs
Female	<3.0 secs	3.0 - 3.3 secs	3.3 - 3.5 secs	3.5 - 3.7 secs	>3.7 secs

These data are for world-class athletes. MACKENZIE, B. (1999) Flying 30 metre Test [WWW] Available from: https://www.brianmac.co.uk/flying30.htm [Accessed 25/5/2023]

Grip dynamometer

Gender	Excellent	Good	Average	Fair	Poor
Male	>56kg	51-56kg	45-50kg	39-44kg	<39kg
Female	>36kg	31-36kg	25-30kg	19-24kg	<19kg

Data for 16-19 year olds. MACKENZIE, B. (2002) Grip Strength Test [WWW] Available from: https://www.brianmac.co.uk/grip.htm [Accessed 30/5/2023]

1RM

Bench press rating	Men aged 20-29	Women aged 20-29
Above average	119kg	54kg
Average	98kg	49kg
Below average	81kg	41kg

American College of Sports Medicine, https://journals.lww.com/acsm-msse/Fulltext/2018/05001/Free_Weight_Bench_Press_Muscular_Fitness_Normative.2026.aspx

BMI

<18.5	18.5–24.9	25–29.9	30-39.9	40<
Underweight	Normal weight	Overweight	Obesity	Extreme Obesity

Waist to hip ratio

rating	male	female
excellent	less than 0.85	less than 0.75
good	0.85-0.89	0.75-0.79
poor	0.90-0.94	0.80-0.84
very poor	above 0.95	above 0.85

MACKENZIE, B. (2008) Waist to Hip Ratio Test [WWW] Available from: https://www.brianmac.co.uk/whrt.htm [Accessed 30/5/2023]

Illinois agility test

Gender	Excellent	Above Average	Average	Below Average	Poor
Male	<15.2 s	15.2 - 16.1 s	16.2 - 18.1 s	18.2 - 19.3 s	>19.3 s
Female	<17.0 s	17.0 - 17.9 s	18.0 - 21.7 s	21.8 - 23.0 s	>23.0 s

MACKENZIE, B. (2000) Illinois Agility Run Test [WWW] Available from: https://www.brianmac.co.uk/illinois.htm [Accessed 1/6/2023]

T test

Female	Number in sample	Result (seconds)
Low sport (G1)	44	13.55 ± 1.33
Recreational sport (G2)	52	12.52 ± 0.90
College athletes (G3)	56	10.94 ± 0.60
Male		
Low sport (G1)	47	11.20 ± 0.80
Recreational sport (G2)	58	10.49 ± 0.89
College athletes (G3)	47	9.94 ± 0.50

PAUOLE KAINOA; MADOLE, KENT; GARHAMMER, JOHN; LACOURSE, MICHAtEL; ROZENEK, RALPH. (2000). Reliability and Validity of the T-Test as a Measure of Agility, Leg Power, and Leg Speed in College-Aged Men and Women. The Journal of Strength & Conditioning Research. 14. 10.1519/00124278-200011000-00012.

Download available at:

https://journals.lww.com/nsca-jscr/Abstract/2000/11000/Reliability_and_Validity_of_the_T_Test_as_a.12.aspx

Stork stand test

Rating	Score (seconds)	
	Men	Women
Advanced	> 51	>28
Advanced Intermediate	37-50	23-27
Intermediate	15-36	8-22
Advanced beginner	5-14	3-7
Beginner	0-4	0-2

Data from Johnson BL, Nelson JK. Practical measurements for evaluation in physical education. 4th Edit. Minneapolis: Burgess, 1979.

Based on scores of 50 men and 50 women at Corpus Christi State University, Texas, in 1976

Available at: https://archive.org/

Y balance test

	Front platform (A)		Right platform (B)		Left platform (C)	
Left or right leg	Left	Right	Left	Right	Left	Right
Absolute Reach (cm)	60.0	59.8	95.7	95.0	91.3	92.1

Normative data from Shaffer et al, 2013; (n = 64 adults 21-29 years of age; Service Members), from: https://www.sralab.org/rehabilitation-measures/lower-quarter-y-balance-test

Alternate hand wall toss test

Rating	Excellent	Good	Average	Fair	Poor
Score (in 30 seconds)	> 35	30 - 35	20- 29	15 - 19	< 15

https://www.topendsports.com/testing/tests/wall-catch.htm

Stick flip test

rating	males (total points)	females (total points)
Excellent	14–15	13–15
Very Good	11–13	10–12
Fair	5–10	4–9
Poor	3–4	2–3
Very Poor	0–2	0–1

https://www.topendsports.com/testing/tests/stick-flip.htm

Vertical jump test

rating	male (cm)	female (cm)
excellent	> 70	> 60
very good	61-70	51-60
above average	51-60	41-50
average	41-50	31-40
below average	31-40	21-30
poor	<31	<21

https://www.topendsports.com/testing/norms/vertical-jump.htm

Standing long/broad jump

rating	Male (cm)	Female (cm)
excellent	> 250	> 200
very good	241-250	191-200
above average	231-240	181-190
average	221-230	171-180
below average	211-220	161-170
poor	<211	<161

https://www.topendsports.com/testing/tests/longjump.htm

Ruler drop test

Rating	Measurement
Excellent	<7.5cm
Above Average	7.5 - 15.9cm
Average	15.9 - 20.4cm
Below Average	20.4 - 28cm
Poor	>28cm

MACKENZIE, B. (2004) Ruler Drop Test [WWW] Available from: https://www.brianmac.co.uk/rulerdrop.htm [Accessed 30/4/2023]

Margaria-Kalamen power test

Men	15-20	21-30	31-40	41-50	Over 50
Excellent	>2,195	>2,058	>1.646	>1,225	>961
Good	1834-2195	1716-2058	1373-1646	1030-1225	805-961
Average	1461-1833	1363-1715	1088-1372	824-1029	638-804
Fair	1107-1460	1039-1,362	833-1088	637-823	490-637
Poor	<1,107	<1,039	<833	<637	<490

Women	15-20	21-30	31-40	41-50	Over 50
Excellent	>1,784	>1,646	>1,225	>961	>736
Good	1481-1784	1373-1646	1029-1225	804-961	599-736
Average	1177-1480	1089-1372	824-1029	638-804	471-598
Fair	902-1176	833-1088	637-823	490-637	372-470
Poor	<902	<833	<637	<490	<372

Based on data from Fox's physiological basis for exercise and sport 6th edition, Foss and Keteyian, McGraw-Hill 1998

Units of measurement in the data tables are Watts (W).

Available at: https://archive.org/details/foxsphysiologica0000foss_6/

Index

A
access to equipment, 189–90
access to venue, 182–90
adaptations, 34, 126–27, 194, 197–99, 202–3
aerobic endurance, 3, 5, 68–69, 122, 134, 140–43, 172, 177, 182–83, 194–95, 200–201
aerobic endurance test, 138–39, 157
aerobic endurance training, 172–73, 194–95
aerobic Zone, 129
alternate-hand wall-toss test, 162
alveoli, 194–95
American football, 33, 43, 71, 95–96, 104
anaerobic system, 129, 172, 182, 187, 199
assistive technology, 34, 41

B
balance, 5, 20–21, 78–79, 125, 160–61, 181, 190, 193, 201
balance test, 161, 212
barriers, 4, 7, 24–27, 41
Barriers to participation and ways, 24–27
baseball, 33, 80, 89, 97, 101, 125, 162, 164
base of support, 78–79, 125, 181
basketball, 29–31, 34–35, 75, 80, 89–90, 92, 95–96, 99, 101–2, 105–6, 164–66, 170, 188
batting sports, 97
beep test, 140
bench press, 132–33, 175, 211
benefits to taking part, 8, 11, 13
BIA machine, 155
biceps, 53–54, 56, 153
blood flow, 170–71
blood vessels, 49, 68, 194–95
BMI, 154

body composition, 22, 73, 124, 154–57
body fat, 73, 155
    amount of, 154–55
body image, 26
body language, 65, 92, 118–19
Body Mass Index, 154
body systems, 194–95, 197, 199
body weight, 59, 70, 153–54, 186
Borg Rating of Perceived Exertion, 130
bowlers, 30–31

C
calf muscle flexibility test, 148
capillaries, 195, 197
capillarisation, 195, 197, 199
cardiac hypertrophy, 194, 199
cardiorespiratory system, 49–50, 52, 57, 61, 68, 172
cardiovascular system, 194
cartilage, 52, 196
centre of mass, 78–79
CHD (coronary heart disease), 21
childcare, 15–16, 25, 191–92
circuit training, 12, 172, 174, 183, 186
closed skills, 81–82
communication, 65, 92, 119
complex skills, 80
components of fitness, 122, 125, 129, 137, 157, 170, 172, 178, 202–3
components of physical fitness, 68–69, 71, 73
components of skill-related fitness, 74–75, 77, 79, 122, 178
conditioned practices, 110–18
continuous training, 172, 182, 200

Cooper test, 143
coordination, 77, 125, 162–63, 178, 189, 199, 201
coronary heart disease (CHD), 21
cricket, 33, 36, 43, 77, 80, 88–90, 97, 100, 102, 125, 162, 164, 169
cycling, 13, 29–30, 33, 37, 90, 98, 140, 182–83

D
Decision Review System (DRS), 43, 90
Delivering a warm-up, 62–63, 65
deltoids, 53–54, 56, 60–61, 153
demonstrations, 63–65, 87, 110, 114–15, 117–18
diabetes, 21–22
drills, 110–11, 114–19, 176, 188–90
DRS (Decision Review System), 43, 90
dynamic balance, 79, 181
dynamic stretch, 54, 57, 61
dynamometer, 152

E
effects of long-term fitness training, 194–95, 197, 199
equipment, sporting, 47
exercise classes, 13
exercise intensity, 5, 52, 57, 128–29, 131, 133, 171–72

F
facilities for sports, 35
fartlek, 172, 183
fencing, 9, 33, 90, 101
fitness programme design, 201, 203
fitness tests, 92, 134–67, 177, 193, 200
fitness training methods for physical components of fitness, 173-177
fitness training methods for skill-related components, 178-181
FITT principles, 126–27, 170, 202
fixed resistance machines, 174–75, 186, 193
flexibility
    calf, 148
    shoulder, 149
fluency, 87
flying sprint test, 151, 157, 210
football, 31–33, 38–39, 42–43, 74, 79–81, 87–88, 92–96, 99–100, 102, 105–6, 108–10, 140–41, 167–68, 178–79, 181–82
Football Association, 8
football boots, 30, 91
football pitch, 42, 93, 101

G
gastrocnemius, 53, 55–56, 60
golf, 98, 100–101
GPS watches, 36, 182, 187, 205

H
hamstrings, 53, 55–56, 60, 147, 153
Harvard Step Test, 142, 157, 208
Hawk-Eye, 45

health benefits of exercise, 23
health conditions, 21, 26, 58, 65
heart, 12, 33, 49, 68, 129, 194
heart rate, 36, 46, 48–49, 52, 57, 128–31, 142, 170–72
heart rate and blood flow, 171
heart rate monitor, 36, 46, 131
hip flexors, 53, 55–56, 60
waist-to-hip ratio test, 156
hockey, 9, 32–33, 61, 75, 88, 91, 100–101, 158, 182

I
ice hockey, 33, 79, 94–96, 100, 107, 183
Illinois agility run test, 158, 169, 211
importance of fitness, 122–23, 125
importance of fitness testing, 134–35, 137, 139
infringements, 88, 90, 102, 105–6
intensity, 3, 48, 50, 57–58, 62, 68, 126, 128, 132–33, 170–72, 199, 202, 207
intensity for muscular endurance, 133
intensity for muscular strength, 132
intervals, 143, 172, 177, 182, 187, 200

J
joints, 51–52, 59–61, 123, 170–71, 188, 190, 196–97
jumping
    horizontal, 164–65
    vertical, 164–65

L
lactic acid, 171, 177, 199
leisure centres, 14–15, 41
ligaments, 50, 72, 196, 198–99
local authorities, 14, 191
long-term fitness training, 5, 194–95, 197, 199
long-term goals, 206–7

M
Margaria-Kalamen power test, 169
mass, fat-free, 155–56
maximum heart rate, 128, 130
mental health, 11, 22–23
minority sport, 15, 17, 191–92
mobiliser, 48, 51–52, 57, 60, 63
motivation, 127, 138, 143, 200, 204–6
motorsport, 38-9, 90, 93
multistage Fitness Test, 140, 208
muscle fatigue, 197
muscle groups, 54, 59, 69–70, 153, 174–75, 185–86, 190
muscle hypertrophy, 198
muscle strength, 181
muscular endurance, 69, 122, 133, 138, 144–46, 174–75, 177, 193, 199, 201
muscular endurance training, 133, 174, 197
muscular strength, 70, 122, 139
musculoskeletal system, 50, 52, 57, 61

N
National Governing Body. See NGB

netball, 31, 60, 82, 88, 90, 96, 104–5, 109, 158, 170, 182
NFL, 43, 104
NGB (National Governing Body), 8, 94, 101

O

obliques, 53, 55–56
officials in sport, 4, 88–89, 91, 93
officials' responsibilities, 91
officiating equipment, 36
online reaction time tests, 167
outdoor activities, 7, 10–12
overload, 126, 186, 198

P

perceived exertion, 46, 130
personal motivation, 200
physical fitness, 4, 68–69, 71, 73, 122
plank, 69, 146
planning a warm-up, 48–57
planning drills and conditioned practices, 110–11, 113–15
plyometrics, 180, 198
PNF, 173, 185
preparation stretch, 53-7
press-ups, 144, 180
principles of training, 173, 202–3
private sector provision, 16–17, 191
protection and safety equipment, 33, 40, 101
providers of sport and physical exercise, 9–19
public sector provision, 14–15
pulse-raiser, 48–50, 52, 59–60, 63, 170–71

Q

quadriceps, 53, 55–56, 60, 153

R

racket sports, 96, 100, 108, 149, 152, 167
recovery time, 158–59
referee, 41, 86, 88, 90, 93, 102, 106–7, 109
regulations, 4, 8, 94–109
resistance drills, 176–77, 188, 193
respiratory muscles, 194–95
respiratory system, 194
reversibility, 127, 202–3
risk of injury, 42, 48, 110, 182–90
rounders, 80, 97, 99
rugby, 29, 31–34, 82–83, 86, 88, 91, 93, 96, 100–101, 140–41, 150, 178–79, 182, 184, 187–88
ruler drop test, 167, 212
rules and regulations, 8, 94, 107
rules and regulations in sport, 94–109

S

safety equipment, 10, 33, 40, 45, 47
SAQ (Speed, Agility and Quickness), 178, 188
short-term goals, 206
sit and reach test, 147
skill-related fitness, 74–79, 124–125, 178–181
skills, 80–83
SMARTER, 205, 207
smartphones, 36, 131, 167
snooker, 95, 98–99
softball, 9, 32–33, 77, 80, 97, 162
specificity, 127, 182–90, 202
Sport England, 14
sporting performance, 116–17, 119
sporting skills, 110–11, 113, 115, 118
sports clothing and equipment, 28-31
sprint test, 151, 157, 210
squash, 31, 33, 47, 75, 95–96, 99
static balance, 78–79, 160, 181
static stretch, 54, 57, 61
strategies and fitness for sports, 4, 80–81, 83, 85, 87
strength and balance activities, 20
strength training, 12, 133, 175, 198
    muscular, 132, 175, 198–99
stretching, 60, 72, 78, 170–71, 173, 177, 196
synovial fluid, 51–52, 170, 196

T

tactics, 44, 84–87, 113
teaching points, 64–65, 115, 118
team sports, 9, 69, 71, 73, 75, 79, 122–23, 182
technology benefits, 37, 39, 41, 43
technology in sport and physical activity, 45, 47
Television Match Official (TMO), 43, 90
tendons, 196
tennis, 31–32, 34, 36, 42–43, 45, 86–88, 95–96, 99, 113, 124–25, 159, 161, 178–79, 181–82, 193
TMO (Television Match Official), 43, 90
touch rugby, 112
training plan, 126–27, 129, 134, 168–69, 177, 203, 205, 207
training sessions, 117, 126–29, 131, 170–71, 202
training zones, 129
triathlons, 28, 35, 122, 157
triceps, 53–54, 56, 60
T-Test, 169, 211

U

umpire, 47, 88–90, 106–8

V

volleyball, 29, 35, 88–89, 95, 100–101, 104–5, 109, 113, 159, 161, 164–66
voluntary sector provision, 16, 191–92

W

warm-ups, 58, 60–61, 63, 110, 170
watersports, 33
wheelchair basketball, 35, 41, 94, 178

Y

Y-balance test, 169
Yo-Yo test, 141, 208

The publisher gratefully acknowledges the permission of copyright holders to reproduce copyright material.

Photograph of the Y-balance test on page 161 reproduced with kind permission from Dr Sheri Sifties, University of South Carolina, from the paper: Silfies SP, Ebaugh D, Pontillo M, Butowicz CM. 'Critical review of the impact of core stability on upper extremity athletic injury and performance'. Braz J Phys Ther. http://dx.doi.org/10.1590/bjpt-rbf.2014.0108

123RF.com: p9 ©shariffc/123RF.COM. p9 ©boggy22/123RF.COM. p9 ©NejroN/123RF.COM.

iStock.com: p88 iStock.com/vm. p88 iStock.com/simonkr. p89 iStock.com/simonkr. p90 iStock.com/lumyaisweet. p91 iStock.com/GlobalStock. p92 iStock.com/FG Trade. p94 iStock.com/nautiluz56. p99 iStock.com/Tashi-Delek. p103 iStock.com/garymilner. p105 iStock.com/SolStock. p105 iStock.com/skynesher. p106 iStock.com/karenfoleyphotography. p109 iStock.com/skynesher. p109 iStock.com/simonkr. p112 iStock.com/RgStudio. p112 iStock.com/DarioGaona. p119 iStock.com/SDI Productions. p119 iStock.com/SolStock. p124 iStock.com/Rudi Silva. p176 iStock.com/SolStock. p178 iStock.com/Georgiy Datsenko. p179 iStock.com/pixdeluxe. p179 iStock.com/AleksandarGeorgiev. p179 iStock.com/CasarsaGuru. p191 iStock.com/Oleksandr Shcherban. p197 iStock.com/Aldona. p198 iStock.com/Gilnature.

Shutterstock.com: p6 Rawpixel.com/Shutterstock. p8 Ivan Smuk/Shutterstock. p9 ©shariffc/123RF.COM. p9 ©boggy22/123RF.COM. p9 ©NejroN/123RF.COM. p9 BearFotos/Shutterstock. p9 Corepics VOF/Shutterstock. p9 Jacob Lund/Shutterstock. p9 matimix/Shutterstock. p9 Monkey Business Images/Shutterstock. p9 Jon Osumi/Shutterstock. p10 PH888/Shutterstock. p10 Ground Picture/Shutterstock. p10 UfaBizPhoto/Shutterstock. p10 Robert Kneschke/Shutterstock. p11 EvgeniiAnd/Shutterstock. p11 Rock and Wasp/Shutterstock. p11 Blazej Lyjak/Shutterstock. p11 Alesia Puzhauskaite/Shutterstock. p12 BearFotos/Shutterstock. p12 karelnoppe/Shutterstock. p12 wavebreakmedia/Shutterstock. p12 NDAB Creativity/Shutterstock. p13 Flotsam/Shutterstock. p13 Goami/Shutterstock. p13 Wachiwit/Shutterstock. p13 Jacob Lund/Shutterstock. p14 BBA Photography/Shutterstock. p16 Jasminko Ibrakovic/Shutterstock. p18 matimix/Shutterstock. p20 stockpexel/Shutterstock. p20 Daisy Daisy/Shutterstock. p21 wavebreakmedia/Shutterstock. p21 BearFotos/Shutterstock. p22 Drazen Zigic/Shutterstock. p22 Lordn/Shutterstock. p23 KieferPix/Shutterstock. p24 Shutters Art/Shutterstock. p24 Shutters Art/Shutterstock. p24 Shutters Art/Shutterstock. p24 Shutters Art/Shutterstock. p25 Chonlatee42/Shutterstock. p25 Alex Tor/Shutterstock. p25 Shutters Art/Shutterstock. p25 Shutters Art/Shutterstock. p25 Shutters Art/Shutterstock. p25 Shutters Art/Shutterstock. p26 Andrey_Popov/Shutterstock. p26 GrooveZ/Shutterstock. p26 Shutters Art/Shutterstock. p26 Shutters Art/Shutterstock. p27 Shutters Art/Shutterstock. p27 Shutters Art/Shutterstock. p28 1 Media/Shutterstock. p28 Maridav/Shutterstock. p28 Nicholas Piccillo/Shutterstock. p28 masik0553/Shutterstock. p29 Asta Zaborskyte/Shutterstock. p29 wk1003mike/Shutterstock. p29 Image Source Trading Ltd/Shutterstock. p29 VitaminCo/Shutterstock. p29 VitaminCo/Shutterstock. p30 Vit Kovalcik/Shutterstock. p30 Sergiy Zavgorodny/Shutterstock. p30 mezzotint/Shutterstock. p30 Alexander Mak/Shutterstock. p30 matimix/Shutterstock. p30 Andriiii/Shutterstock. p31 Maridav/Shutterstock. p31 Lipik Stock Media/Shutterstock. p32 Dean Drobot/Shutterstock. p32 Liderina/Shutterstock. p32 SEALANDSKYPHOTO/Shutterstock. p32 stockphoto-graf/Shutterstock. p32 Rafa artphoto/Shutterstock. p33 calden jamieson/Shutterstock. p33 BLACKDAY/Shutterstock. p33 Hero Images Inc/Shutterstock. p33 Flowersandtraveling/Shutterstock. p33 Melinda Nagy/Shutterstock. p34 KONSTANTIN_SHISHKIN/Shutterstock. p34 Gorodenkoff/Shutterstock. p34 KOTOIMAGES/Shutterstock. p34 artichoke studio/Shutterstock. p35 J. Helgason/Shutterstock. p35 Pavel1964/Shutterstock. p36 roibu/Shutterstock. p36 ra2 studio/Shutterstock. p37 lanastace/Shutterstock. p37 Real Sports Photos/Shutterstock. p37 MarySan/Shutterstock. p38 Peyker/Shutterstock. p38 ID1974/Shutterstock. p38 OSTILL is Franck Camhi/Shutterstock. p39 Haslam Photography/Shutterstock. p40 wavebreakmedia/Shutterstock. p40 niteenrk/Shutterstock. p40 Andrey Burmakin/Shutterstock. p41 Sergey Granev/Shutterstock. p41 Pressmaster/Shutterstock. p41 NassornSnitwong/Shutterstock. p42 CHAINFOTO24/Shutterstock. p42 TORWAISTUDIO/Shutterstock. p42 sagulpol2807/Shutterstock. p42 Polhansen/Shutterstock. p43 Supermop/Shutterstock. p43 Naypong Studio/Shutterstock. p44 Maridav/Shutterstock. p44 metamorworks/Shutterstock. p45 Diki Prayogo/Shutterstock. p45 mbezvodinskikh/Shutterstock. p46 BigNazik/Shutterstock. p46 Eakrin Rasadonyindee/Shutterstock. p48 natiavektor/Shutterstock. p48 natiavektor/Shutterstock. p48 Lio putra/Shutterstock. p48 Lio putra/Shutterstock. p48 Lio putra/Shutterstock. p48 Lio putra/Shutterstock. p48 Lio putra/Shutterstock. p48 Lio putra/Shutterstock. p48 Lio putra/Shutterstock. p49 Creativa Images/Shutterstock. p49 LoopAll/Shutterstock. p49 LoopAll/Shutterstock. p50 Kjpargeter/Shutterstock. p51 Lio putra/Shutterstock. p51 Lio putra/Shutterstock. p51 Lio putra/Shutterstock. p51 Lio putra/Shutterstock. p51 solar22/Shutterstock. p51 Lio putra/Shutterstock. p51 Lio putra/Shutterstock. p51 Lio putra/Shutterstock. p51 Lio putra/Shutterstock. p52 joshya/Shutterstock. p52 PanicAttack/Shutterstock. p53 MadiGraphic/Shutterstock. p53 Hank Grebe/Shutterstock. p53 TreesTons/Shutterstock. p54 Lio putra/Shutterstock. p55 Lio putra/Shutterstock. p56 Lio putra/Shutterstock. p57 Melodia plus photos/Shutterstock. p57 wavebreakmedia/Shutterstock. p57 Master1305/Shutterstock. p57 TreesTons/Shutterstock. p58 Ground Picture/Shutterstock. p59 Kzenon/Shutterstock. p60 Juice Flair/Shutterstock. p60 marinat197/Shutterstock. p62 BAZA Production/Shutterstock. p63 Valmedia/Shutterstock. p63 DGLimages/Shutterstock. p64 PeopleImages.com - Yuri A/Shutterstock. p66 sutadimages/Shutterstock. p68 zuperia/Shutterstock. p68 zuperia/Shutterstock. p68 LoopAll/Shutterstock. p68 LoopAll/Shutterstock. p68 Real Sports Photos/Shutterstock. p68 SciePro/Shutterstock. p69 rangizzz/Shutterstock. p69 Friends Stock/Shutterstock. p70 Aleksey Mnogosmyslov/Shutterstock. p70 Air Images/Shutterstock. p70 Makatserchyk/Shutterstock. p70 Real Sports Photos/Shutterstock. p70 AerialVision_it/Shutterstock. p71 taka1022/Shutterstock. p71 PabloBenii/Shutterstock. p71 William Farquhar/Shutterstock. p71 Daniel Padavona/Shutterstock. p72 Roka Pics/Shutterstock. p72 Air Images/Shutterstock. p72 Master1305/Shutterstock. p72 AT Production/Shutterstock. p73 lzf/Shutterstock. p74 Valeriy Velikov/Shutterstock. p74 PeopleImages.com - Yuri A/Shutterstock. p74 wavebreakmedia/Shutterstock. p75 dotshock/Shutterstock. p75 sirtravelalot/Shutterstock. p75 taka1022/Shutterstock. p76 Pavel1964/Shutterstock. p76 Valeriy

Velikov/Shutterstock. p76 Valeriy Velikov/Shutterstock. p77 Juice Flair/Shutterstock. p77 ChrisVanLennepPhoto/Shutterstock. p77 PeopleImages.com - Yuri A/Shutterstock. p77 LightField Studios/Shutterstock. p78 wavebreakmedia/Shutterstock. p79 Dmity Trush/Shutterstock. p79 Gorodenkoff/Shutterstock. p79 Alena Ozerova/Shutterstock. p80 Kingmaya Studio/Shutterstock. p80 Dean Clarke/Shutterstock. p80 Stefan Schurr/Shutterstock. p81 Dewald Kirsten/Shutterstock. p81 makieni/Shutterstock. p81 Robert J. Beyers II/Shutterstock. p81 vlalukinv/Shutterstock. p82 Real Sports Photos/Shutterstock. p82 dotshock/Shutterstock. p82 Olga Vladimirova/Shutterstock. p82 Dziurek/Shutterstock. p83 inspiring.team/Shutterstock. p83 OtmarW/Shutterstock. p83 wavebreakmedia/Shutterstock. p83 Gorodenkoff/Shutterstock. p84 ErebrorMountain/Shutterstock. p85 sirtravelalot/Shutterstock. p86 PeopleImages.com - Yuri A/Shutterstock. p86 SumanBhaumik/Shutterstock. p86 PeopleImages.com - Yuri A/Shutterstock. p89 Lance Bellers/Shutterstock. p90 sirtravelalot/Shutterstock. p92 WoodysPhotos/Shutterstock. p93 voronaman/Shutterstock. p93 Ristovski Dragan/Shutterstock. p94 daykung/Shutterstock. p94 Aleksandr Lupin/Shutterstock. p95 Pavel K/Shutterstock. p96 Scott's Shotz Photography/Shutterstock. p96 Torychemistry/Shutterstock. p97 Lance Bellers/Shutterstock. p97 Real Sports Photos/Shutterstock. p98 Belish/Shutterstock. p98 BadPixma/Shutterstock. p100 Inna Tan/Shutterstock. p100 HappyPictures/Shutterstock. p100 LeKoKo/Shutterstock. p100 phoelixDE/Shutterstock. p101 calden jamieson/Shutterstock. p101 Rawpixel.com/Shutterstock. p103 Monkey Business Images/Shutterstock. p103 Damiano Buffo/Shutterstock. p105 wavebreakmedia/Shutterstock. p106 Gorodenkoff/Shutterstock. p107 Image Source Collection/Shutterstock. p107 Thomas Heden/Shutterstock. p108 roibu/Shutterstock. p108 hrk422/Shutterstock. p108 DexonDee/Shutterstock. p110 matimix/Shutterstock. p110 noomcpk/Shutterstock. p111 Drazen Zigic/Shutterstock. p111 matimix/Shutterstock. p113 Mr.Note19/Shutterstock. p113 Olena Yakobchuk/Shutterstock. p114 Rawpixel.com/Shutterstock. p114 serhii.suravikin/Shutterstock. p115 Damiano Buffo/Shutterstock. p116 WoodysPhotos/Shutterstock. p116 Andrii Medvednikov/Shutterstock. p117 Monkey Business Images/Shutterstock. p118 ALPA PROD/Shutterstock. p118 matimix/Shutterstock. p120 koonsiri boonnak/Shutterstock. p122 Pavel1964/Shutterstock. p122 videoTD/Shutterstock. p122 Maridav/Shutterstock. p122 Pressmaster/Shutterstock. p122 blurAZ/Shutterstock. p123 TORWAISTUDIO/Shutterstock. p123 Jacob Lund/Shutterstock. p123 Air Images/Shutterstock. p123 Real Sports Photos/Shutterstock. p123 wavebreakmedia/Shutterstock. p123 Corepics VOF/Shutterstock. p124 makieni/Shutterstock. p124 Real Sports Photos/Shutterstock. p124 Inside Creative House/Shutterstock. p125 wavebreakmedia/Shutterstock. p125 matimix/Shutterstock. p125 Suzanne Tucker/Shutterstock. p126 Microgen/Shutterstock. p127 Mongkolchon Akesin/Shutterstock. p128 Ground Picture/Shutterstock. p128 tawanroong/Shutterstock. p130 ThirtyPlus/Shutterstock. p131 DenPhotos/Shutterstock. p131 BallBall14/Shutterstock. p131 Maridav/Shutterstock. p132 BGStock72/Shutterstock. p133 WeStudio/Shutterstock. p134 Jacob Lund/Shutterstock. p134 Gorodenkoff/Shutterstock. p134 Prostock-studio/Shutterstock. p135 michaeljung/Shutterstock. p135 Tetiana Rostopira/Shutterstock. p135 Andrei Kuzmik/Shutterstock. p137 Goami/Shutterstock. p138 ThirtyPlus/Shutterstock. p138 Drazen Zigic/Shutterstock. p139 Gorodenkoff/Shutterstock. p139 PeopleImages.com - Yuri A/Shutterstock. p139 ra2 studio/Shutterstock. p140 Lova Mikhailova/Shutterstock. p140 Inate/Shutterstock. p140 Inate/Shutterstock. p141 Lova Mikhailova/Shutterstock. p141 Fotokostic/Shutterstock. p141 Inate/Shutterstock. p141 Inate/Shutterstock. p141 Inate/Shutterstock. p142 Parkheta/Shutterstock. p143 Pavel L Photo and Video/Shutterstock. p144 Lio putra/Shutterstock. p144 Lio putra/Shutterstock. p145 Lio putra/Shutterstock. p145 Lio putra/Shutterstock. p146 Lio putra/Shutterstock. p147 Microgen/Shutterstock. p148 Lio putra/Shutterstock. p148 Lio putra/Shutterstock. p149 Lio putra/Shutterstock. p150 Inate/Shutterstock. p150 Inate/Shutterstock. p151 Inate/Shutterstock. p151 Inate/Shutterstock. p151 Inate/Shutterstock. p152 Microgen/Shutterstock. p153 Lio putra/Shutterstock. p154 Vaillery/Shutterstock. p155 Joyisjoyful/Shutterstock. p156 Avilika/Shutterstock. p157 Lio putra/Shutterstock. p157 Lio putra/Shutterstock. p157 Inate/Shutterstock. p157 Inate/Shutterstock. p157 Inate/Shutterstock. p162 Lio putra/Shutterstock. p162 gomolach/Shutterstock. p162 NiRain/Shutterstock. p165 Lio putra/Shutterstock. p166 Dragon Images/Shutterstock. p167 Microgen/Shutterstock. p168 PeopleImages.com - Yuri A/Shutterstock. p168 Ali DM/Shutterstock. p169 Ali DM/Shutterstock. p170 Odua Images/Shutterstock. p171 pisitbz/Shutterstock. p171 Dragon Images/Shutterstock. p172 Basilico Studio Stock/Shutterstock. p173 Air Images/Shutterstock. p173 fizkes/Shutterstock. p173 Lio putra/Shutterstock. p174 wavebreakmedia/Shutterstock. p174 Ground Picture/Shutterstock. p174 TORWAISTUDIO/Shutterstock. p174 Boris Rabtsevich/Shutterstock. p174 Boris Rabtsevich/Shutterstock. p174 Boris Rabtsevich/Shutterstock. p174 Boris Rabtsevich/Shutterstock. p174 Drazen Zigic/Shutterstock. p175 RatcStock/Shutterstock. p175 RatcStock/Shutterstock. p175 Ground Picture/Shutterstock. p175 Lyashenko Egor/Shutterstock. p176 matimix/Shutterstock. p176 PH888/Shutterstock. p178 DisobeyArt/Shutterstock. p178 Nattawit Khomsanit/Shutterstock. p178 nazarovsergey/Shutterstock. p179 Jacob Lund/Shutterstock. p179 Macrovector/Shutterstock. p180 Lio putra/Shutterstock. p180 Lio putra/Shutterstock. p180 Lio putra/Shutterstock. p180 Lio putra/Shutterstock. p180 Lio putra/Shutterstock. p181 solar22/Shutterstock. p181 solar22/Shutterstock. p181 Alliance Images/Shutterstock. p181 solar22/Shutterstock. p191 wavebreakmedia/Shutterstock. p192 Blan-k/Shutterstock. p194 first vector trend/Shutterstock. p194 SciePro/Shutterstock. p195 BlueRingMedia/Shutterstock. p195 Sakurra/Shutterstock. p196 Maridav/Shutterstock. p196 Olga Bolbot/Shutterstock. p198 KurArt/Shutterstock. p199 Inside Creative House/Shutterstock. p200 Ground Picture/Shutterstock. p201 Master1305/Shutterstock. p202 DC Studio/Shutterstock. p202 Gorodenkoff/Shutterstock. p202 Iammotos/Shutterstock. p203 Ground Picture/Shutterstock. p203 Bojan Milinkov/Shutterstock. p203 EpicStockMedia/Shutterstock. p204 Tartila/Shutterstock. p204 Northern Owl/Shutterstock. p204 Dhaka Vector Studio/Shutterstock. p204 Yefym Turkin/Shutterstock. p205 3DMAVR/Shutterstock. p206 Generative AI/Shutterstock. p206 Drazen Zigic/Shutterstock. p207 PeopleImages.com - Yuri A/Shutterstock. p211 Pikovit/Shutterstock.